Cambridge Elements

Elements in Construction Grammar
edited by
Thomas Hoffmann
Catholic University of Eichstätt-Ingolstadt
Alexander Bergs
Osnabrück University

MULTIMODAL CONSTRUCTION GRAMMAR

Elisabeth Zima
University of Freiburg

Shaftesbury Road, Cambridge CB2 8EA, United Kingdom

One Liberty Plaza, 20th Floor, New York, NY 10006, USA

477 Williamstown Road, Port Melbourne, VIC 3207, Australia

314–321, 3rd Floor, Plot 3, Splendor Forum, Jasola District Centre, New Delhi – 110025, India

103 Penang Road, #05–06/07, Visioncrest Commercial, Singapore 238467

Cambridge University Press is part of Cambridge University Press & Assessment, a department of the University of Cambridge.

We share the University's mission to contribute to society through the pursuit of education, learning and research at the highest international levels of excellence.

www.cambridge.org
Information on this title: www.cambridge.org/9781009571746

DOI: 10.1017/9781009359856

© Elisabeth Zima 2025

This publication is in copyright. Subject to statutory exception and to the provisions of relevant collective licensing agreements, no reproduction of any part may take place without the written permission of Cambridge University Press & Assessment.

When citing this work, please include a reference to the DOI 10.1017/9781009359856

First published 2025

A catalogue record for this publication is available from the British Library

ISBN 978-1-009-57174-6 Hardback
ISBN 978-1-009-35987-0 Paperback
ISSN 2753-2674 (online)
ISSN 2753-2666 (print)

Cambridge University Press & Assessment has no responsibility for the persistence or accuracy of URLs for external or third-party internet websites referred to in this publication and does not guarantee that any content on such websites is, or will remain, accurate or appropriate.

For EU product safety concerns, contact us at Calle de José Abascal, 56, 1°, 28003 Madrid, Spain, or email eugpsr@cambridge.org

Multimodal Construction Grammar

Elements in Construction Grammar

DOI: 10.1017/9781009359856
First published online: August 2025

Elisabeth Zima
University of Freiburg

Author for correspondence: Elisabeth Zima, elisabeth.zima@germanistik.uni-freiburg.de

Abstract: This Element in Construction Grammar addresses one of its hottest topics and asks: is the unimodal conception of Construction Grammar as a model of linguistic knowledge at odds with the usage-based thesis and the multimodality of language use? Are constructions verbal, i.e. unimodal form-meaning pairings, or are they, or at least are some of them, multimodal in nature? And, more fundamentally, how do we know? These questions have been debated quite controversially over the past few years. This Element presents the current state of research within the field, paying special attention to the arguments that are put forward in favour and against the uni-/multimodal nature of constructions and the various case studies that have been conducted. Although significant progress has been made over the years, the debate points towards a need for a diversification of the questions asked, the data studied, and the methods used to analyse these data.

Keywords: Construction Grammar, gaze, gesture, multimodal constructions, multimodal packages, multimodality, prosody, recurrence, statistical methods

© Elisabeth Zima 2025

ISBNs: 9781009571746 (HB), 9781009359870 (PB), 9781009359856 (OC)
ISSNs: 2753-2674 (online), 2753-2666 (print)

Contents

1 Introduction — 1

2 Theoretical Preliminaries — 4

3 Ways to Model the Multimodality of Constructions — 10

4 Studies in Multimodal Construction Grammar — 16

5 Interactional Research on Multimodal Packages — 27

6 Beyond Gestures: Gaze and Prosody — 30

7 The Future: Where Do We Go from Here? — 40

8 Concluding Remarks — 48

References — 50

1 Introduction

Human language use is, for the most part, multimodal in nature. From the moment of birth, individuals are immersed in a multimodal environment in which people engage and communicate with each other through verbal language, sounds, gestures, facial expressions, postures, gazes, and other non-verbal resources. As humans, we possess unique cognitive capacities to process the incoming stream of information and to integrate it into holistic meanings to arrive at coherent understandings of the situations at hand. At the same time, our cognitive abilities allow us to communicate multimodally ourselves, conveying information in multiple modalities simultaneously. In this multimodal in- and output, verbal language plays a primordial role due to its unmatched semiotic complexity. Nonetheless, non-verbal communication is more than just 'decoration' to the verbally conveyed messages. In gesture studies, kinesic expressive means, such as, for instance, facial expressions and manual gestures, have long been advocated to be not only inherently meaningful but part and parcel of language (McNeill, 1985, 1992; Kendon, 2004; Karadöller, Sümer & Özyürek, 2024).

However, the conception of language as intrinsically multimodal is not the mainstream view in linguistics in general and Construction Grammar (CxG) in particular. Like all linguistic theories and models of grammar, CxG emerged from the study of verbal – that is, unimodal and mostly written – language and was designed as a framework to account for the inventory of linguistic form–meaning pairings that are taken to constitute languages as systems (Cappelle, 2024: 42). Multimodality did not play a role in its development until very recently. My primary aim in this Element is to put this unimodal focus on language into question and to delve into the consequences that result from the multimodality of language use for how we conceptualise languages as systems and conceive of constructions as their constituents. In doing so, I give prominence to one of the most recent and contentiously debated issues in CxG and ask whether constructions are, or at least can be, multimodal. This inevitably raises the follow-up question of whether we must reconceptualise the model of Construction Grammar as a multimodal model, and what this would mean for how we model constructions and the relations between them. Note that the focus of this Element will be on spoken language, but I will occasionally also include perspectives from sign language research and research on speech/text/image multimodality, as, for example, in memes.

A growing body of work (i.a. Andrén, 2010; Cienki, 2015, 2016; Zima, 2017; Debras, 2021; Uhrig, 2021a, 2021b, 2022; Lehmann & Pentrel, 2023; Lehmann, 2024), including a recent monograph (Schoonjans, 2018), a special issue (Zima & Bergs, 2017), a collective volume by Fried and Nikiforidou (2025), and a chapter in *The Cambridge Handbook of Construction Grammar* (Zima 2025), testify to the growing interest in the potential ramifications of adopting a multimodal perspective on language use, constructionhood, and the language system.[1] This Element thus enters new and exciting ground. Given the newness of the field and the fundamental nature of the questions that arise from taking a multimodal perspective, the tone, however, will be rather tentative and I will strive to provide a nuanced perspective on the topic, arguing less in terms of 'this is a multimodal construction and this is not' but drawing attention to what we could and should do to advance the topic. This cautiousness mirrors the fact that studying constructs in their natural multimodal environment with the aim of identifying multimodal constructions is a complex undertaking. It is not only faced with the manifold issues that verbally orientated CxG also struggles with, such as different takes on the role of frequency of (co)-occurrence and whether it is considered to indicate constructionhood or not (see also, most recently, Ungerer & Hartmann, 2023: 47). Most notably, multimodality brings in a range of new issues that lay beyond the traditional scope of most (Construction) Grammarians.

One of them, for instance, relates to the temporal intricacies of multimodal language use in face-to-face interaction, as non-verbal meaning aspects may not always be perfectly synchronised with their verbal correlates (or affiliates) or operate on different timescales altogether. Another challenge is set by the variance that is intrinsic to multimodal utterances, which urges us to take a broader stance on the nature of recurrence. I will argue that to book progress in the field, it is not sufficient to look out for recurrent co-occurrences of verbal, para-verbal, or non-verbal forms, although this may be a necessary first step to take. Rather, research in Multimodal Construction Grammar crucially hinges on a thorough understanding of the complex nature of multimodal interaction and sense-making. This entails that as Construction Grammarians, we need to genuinely broaden our purely linguistic – that is, verbally centred – perspectives and take a holistic view on language (in) use. This includes weighing different factors that may impact why speakers use given non-verbal signs together with verbal constructions in particular moments in interaction, or more broadly, combine visual and auditory signals to form meaning units in embodied, situated language use. In doing so, it is essential to consider the semiotic import of kinesic articulators. In a similar vein, however, it is equally essential to bear in mind that the functions of non-verbal cues are not always semantically related to the meaning of the ongoing utterance (part) they co-occur with. For example, a given gaze behaviour that accompanies a given construction may serve a floor management function rather than being tightly linked on a semantic level with the construction with which it is temporally synchronised.

---

[1] *The Cambridge Handbook of Construction Grammar* appeared after completion of this Element. Therefore, the work published in it could not be taken into consideration.

Understanding the intricacies of multimodal interaction and its management is hence an indispensable prerequisite to any theorising about the multimodality of constructions and the constructicon. For decades, the nature of social interaction in all its contexts and dimensions has been the focus of investigation in neighbouring disciplines such as Conversation Analysis (CA), Interactional Linguistics (IL), and Gesture Studies. Taking CxG to the realm of multimodality can be a fruitful endeavour only if analyses and conclusions are compatible with the acquired wisdom in these fields. Of course, this does not entail that (all) Construction Grammarians need to become experts in CA or gesture studies, but cooperation and the will to go beyond the traditional focus of the field are imperative.

At the same time, at least some versions of Construction Grammar argue that constructions are real cognitive entities – that is, mental representations that are entrenched in language users' minds (Goldberg, 2003; for a discussion, see Cappelle, 2024: 3). Consequently, it is equally mandatory to ground findings, arguments, and claims in what we know about the cognitive processes that drive the production and understanding of multimodal language use. This entails that we need to orient towards the cognitive sciences to make sure that our conception of multimodal grammar is compatible with what we know about multimodal language production and processing.

The need for interdisciplinarity and to see beyond one's own nose is not the least crucial to counter recent claims according to which Construction Grammar is an 'anything-goes approach' and no solid criteria exist for asserting constructionhood (Cappelle, 2024: 12). It becomes especially eminent in the context of multimodal language use because, as (Cienki, 2017: 1) has argued, the complexity and natural variance of the data bring some issues and theoretical debates of CxG to the fore with even greater saliency than in 'unimodal CxG'.

Before we dive deeper into the topic and start with why multimodality is a core issue for usage-based linguistic approaches such as CxG in Section 2, note that the growing interest in the identification of multimodal units in discourse is not a trend that is unique to CxG. Recent conversation analytical and interactional linguistic work has focussed on very similar issues, trying to identify recurrent configurations of verbal and non-verbal conduct in interactional data. These multimodal configurations have received different name tags, including *multimodal packages* (Stukenbrock, 2010; Balantani, 2022), *multimodal assemblies* (Pekarek Doehler, 2019), *multimodal Gestalts* (Mondada, 2014, 2024), *multimodal social action formats* (Pekarek Doehler, 2022), and *syntactic-bodily units* (Keevallik, 2020). The findings made in this line of research, as well as the issues and concerns raised, are highly relevant for Multimodal Construction Grammar and will therefore also receive attention in this Element (Section 5). However, before that, we need to lay the epistemological ground for the discussion. We start with the very basic observations that the primary locus for language use is *face-to-face* interaction, and *face-to-face* interaction is inherently multimodal in nature.

2 Theoretical Preliminaries

2.1 *Face-to-Face* Interaction Is Primordial and Language Use Is Multimodal

From both an ontogenetic and a phylogenetic perspective, *face-to-face* interaction stands out from other forms of human interaction and communication. Not only did human communication and language evolve from *face-to-face* interaction and are languages learnt through the interaction with other humans in direct, focussed interaction with co-present interactants, but *face-to-face* interaction is the primary locus of human socialisation tout court. It is through direct, embodied interactions with others that we learn to 'be human', as Cooperrider (2009: 373) argues: 'face-to-face interaction is the foundation of human social life ... it's where we learn a language, a culture, a way of being human'. The ontogenetic significance of *face-to-face* interaction is crucially derived from the fact that children learn all the basic rules and norms of social coexistence and cooperation in and through interaction with others. Moreover, it is the central locus of (early) childhood language acquisition.

Its fundamental importance is, however, by no means restricted to the early years. Rather, *face-to-face* interaction is the natural habitat of language throughout the entire lifespan, or as Holler, Kendrick, and Levinson (2018: 1900) put it most poignantly: it is 'the home of human language use'.[2] Neither the development of writing nor technical achievements such as the invention of the telephone or the various forms of computer-mediated interaction (videoconferencing, email, chat, WhatsApp, or social media) have fundamentally changed the role of *face-to-face* interaction for human sociality and communication: 'face-to-face interaction is still primal and primary' (Turner, 2002: 1).

A fundamental characteristic of human *face-to-face* interaction is its multimodality (Karadöller, Sümer & Özyürek, 2024: 1). This term refers to the fact that in human communication, meaning is conveyed simultaneously in a wide range of semiotic channels including verbal language, hand and head gestures, facial gestures, gaze, body postures, and body positioning, as well as proxemics – that is, the spatial interrelationship between interactants. Therefore, utterances are semiotically complex structures that emerge from the interaction of

---

[2] In a similar vein, Perniss (2018: 1) talks about the 'primary ecological niche of language'; for similar quotes, see Schegloff (1987: 102), Goodwin (2003: 57), and Meyer (2016: 1).

different modalities in situ (in the sense of Enfield 2009, who coined the term 'composite utterances').

This has long been understood and taken for granted in Conversation Analysis where social interaction was considered an inherently multimodal phenomenon from early on. However, the recognition of the multimodality of social interaction was of a theoretical kind and work in CA was long characterised by a strong, even exclusive focus on the verbal channel (see also Auer, 2021; Kendrick, Holler & Levinson, 2023). This includes groundbreaking work, such as that by Sacks, Schegloff, and Jefferson (1974) on the turn-taking system. It was not until the 2000s that a genuine multimodal turn set in, which was not the least stipulated by the improved possibilities of recording and analysing multimodal data. However, some early pioneering studies explicitly focussed on multimodal aspects. This includes work by Kendon (1967) and several studies by Charles Goodwin (1980, 1981; Goodwin & Goodwin, 1986) on the role of gaze for turn-taking management, as well as studies by Streeck and Hartge (1992), Heath (1993), and Streeck (1993) with reference to co-verbal gestures.

Usage-based linguistics is fully compatible with CA in acknowledging that language use is fundamentally multimodal. It has long been recognised that the primary setting of language, or its *ur*-context (Cienki, 2016: 605), is *face-to-face* interaction. However, also in Cognitive Linguistics, the multimodality of language use has long been nothing more than a theoretical given that was of little actual significance to the development of the field. It is only a fairly recent trend that Cognitive Linguists have started to fully embrace the multimodal nature of language use by working with authentic, video-recorded discursive data and developing theories to account for how semiotic modes work together in conceptualisation.

A serious boost for multimodality research from a CL perspective came from pioneer studies on multimodal metaphor and metonymy as expressed in co-speech gesture (Mittelberg, 2006, 2019; Cienki, 2008; Cienki & Müller, 2008; Müller, 2008) as well as in pictures and video (Forceville, 2008; for an overview, see Sanaz, 2013; Feyaerts, Brône & Oben, 2017). Over the past decade, other Cognitive Linguistic paradigms have followed that path and widened their focus towards the kinesic modalities. Most notably and of central importance to our discussion here, some Construction Grammarians have raised the issue of whether, in the light of the inherent multimodality of human language use, the status of constructions as pairings of verbal forms and verbally encoded meanings may have to be reconsidered (Andrén, 2010; Cienki, 2015, 2016; Dancygier & Vandelanotte, 2017; Feyaerts, Brône & Oben, 2017; Zima, 2017, Zima & Bergs, 2017; Schoonjans, 2018; Ungerer & Hartmann, 2023).

At the same time, interactional linguists and gesture researchers have turned to Construction Grammar in search of a model of linguistic knowledge and cognitive representation to account for the tied coupling of verbal and kinesic structures observed in language use (Lanwer, 2017; Stukenbrock, 2020; Debras, 2021). This convergent development originated at the very core of the usage-based model and its premise that all knowledge of language is abstracted from language use.

However, the implications of fully embracing the multimodality of language use are far-reaching for Cognitive Linguistics. Most notably, it raises the question of 'what counts as language' (Cienki, 2016: 606; see also Ladewig 2020 and Cohn & Schilperoord 2024 for similar arguments) and therefore what the research objects of Cognitive Linguistics should be. Furthermore, as I will show in Sections 3 and 4, many theoretical debates that are ongoing within the field (for in-depth, state-of-the-art overviews, see Ungerer & Hartmann, 2023; Capelle, 2024) become even more intricate if one leaves behind the artificial reduction of communicative signals to its verbal parts (Schoonjans, 2017).

Multimodal communication is semiotically complex, extremely fast, and yet, most of the time, unproblematic to produce and to decode for the human mind. While processing multimodal interaction, the task of the recipient's mind is highly complex, as it needs not only to differentiate semantically meaningful bodily behaviour from incidental or self-adaptive movements, such as scratching the neck or fiddling with one's wedding ring, but also to integrate the bulk of the incoming semiotic information to generate the meanings of utterances. This multimodal stream of information that recipients must process – and respond to in due time! – is not always neatly aligned on a temporal level. It is, for instance, well known that manual gestures usually precede their lexical affiliate in time (if there is one) and also nods and other head movements often do not neatly coincide with their verbal counterparts on a temporal level. Furthermore, the lexical affiliate need not be one word or one syntactic constituent but may involve a much larger unit of discourse. While the human mind has no problem dealing with these issues, they pose serious challenges to Multimodal Construction Grammar as the concept of 'co-occurrence' cannot simply be translated into 'temporal synchronicity'.

However, these are not only issues that Construction Grammarians struggle with, but they are equally consequential for conversation analytical and interactional linguistic work on recurrent combinations of verbal and kinesic form, as we will see in Section 5. Before that, however, we turn to the most important reason for why the idea of Multimodal Construction Grammar came into being in the first place: the usage-based thesis.

2.2 Multimodality and the Usage-Based Thesis

Usage-based approaches model grammar as 'the cognitive organization of one's experience with language' (Bybee, 2006: 2916). Consequently, CxG is 'a theory of what speakers know when they know a language, that is, when they know how to produce and process language' (Hilpert, 2021: 4ff.). Construction Grammarians have taken this claim further to posit that language in its entirety consists of constructions. This idea is reminiscent of Goldberg's (2003: 226) iconic statement: 'It's constructions all the way down' and of Hilpert's (2014: 2) phrasing: 'knowledge of language consists of a large network of constructions, *and nothing else in addition* ' (my emphasis) (see also Hilpert, 2021: 6).

'Construction' is an evolving concept (Ungerer & Hartmann, 2023: 5), but the core idea has remained stable over the years: Constructions are considered to be symbolic units of language that are abstracted from language use as recurrent associations between forms and meanings. This is captured in the representation of the usage-based cycle in Figure 1. It depicts the core assumption that schemas (or constructions (A)) are abstracted from concrete instances of language use (B) based on recurrent commonalities. These schemas, in turn, serve as templates for language use (C).

It follows from the fact that the natural habitat of language is multimodal *face-to-face* interaction that constructions typically are stored abstractions of form–function commonalities observed in multimodal language use.[3] This statement surely is uncontroversial since it does not make any assumptions about the semiotic complexity of the stored patterns – that is, their unimodal or multimodal structure. It is equally uncontroversial in CxG that constructions are connected to each other in a network, the so-called constructicon, although there may not be full consensus on the details of the network (Diessel, 2023). Furthermore, there are different, interrelated but not congruent dimensions to constructions and the constructicon: both concepts are used to refer both to the systems of conventionalised signs that are shared among members of speech communities and the mental representation of individuals. The very fact that

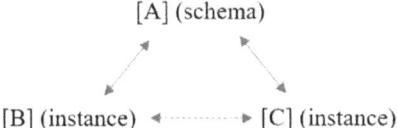

Figure 1 The usage-based cycle (adapted from Langacker, 1987: 373).

---

[3] Note that the same usage-based cycle of language use and the abstraction of units also applies to constructions of written language and iconographic symbols such as, for instance, emoticons.

these systems of knowledge need to overlap so as to make interpersonal communication possible is evident, but entrenchment and conventionalisation are by no means just two sides of the same coin (Schmid, 2014). Nevertheless, for the time being, we leave this issue aside and concentrate on the argument that seems to be implicit in Hilpert's all-encompassing view of constructions and the constructicon: if it is constructions and nothing else in addition, knowledge of constructions as assembled in the constructicon must inevitably include knowledge on how to instantiate them multimodally. This is in agreement with the line of thinking that I have put forward in Zima (2014): if we go with the idea that the constructicon captures all our knowledge of language, we have a hard time conceptualising language and constructions as purely unimodal – that is, verbal in nature – as we are left with a twofold problem. First, we would have to be able to explain why the usage-based thesis should hold for recurrences at the verbal level only and not for recurrences in non-verbal modalities. Ultimately, this would imply assuming that verbal language is acquired differently than knowledge on non-verbal communication. It is doubtful that many usage-based linguists would subscribe to this idea, as it is at odds with the fundamental premise of CL that language learning is not domain-specific (Bybee, 2002). This leads to the question of where our knowledge of how to communicate multimodally – that is, how to act as a competent interactant in natural, multimodal conversations – is stored and why it is stored separately from verbal language.

Another take on the issue is to view grammar and language knowledge as non-equivalent (see Bybee, just cited, who talks about grammar and not language). According to that view, knowledge of language is more encompassing and includes grammatical knowledge as one of its components. In other words, constructions are conceptualised as *grammatical* units that constitute grammar, whereas language is more than grammar. Consequently, it contains more than just constructions. We will come back to this issue in Section 3, where we focus on the different approaches to multimodality within the CxG framework.

But let us step back for a moment and call to mind that the discussion of where in the CxG model one needs to locate recurrent non-verbal cues did not originate in CxG. Rather, it was stipulated by Ronald Langacker, who explicitly acknowledged that gestures may be part of linguistic units.

> In Cognitive Grammar ..., the form in a form-meaning pairing is specifically phonological structure. I would of course generalize this to include other symbolizing media, notably gesture and writing. ... Cognitive Grammar takes the straightforward position that *any* aspect of a usage event, or even a sequence of usage events in a discourse, is capable of emerging as a linguistic unit, should it be a recurrent commonality. (Langacker, 2001: 146, author's emphasis)

In 2008, he even got more specific, giving the example of a co-speech gesture that is performed in baseball:

> When a baseball empire yells Safe! And simultaneously gives the standard gestural signal to this effect (raising both arms together to shoulder level and then sweeping the hands outward, palms down), why should only the former be analysed as part of the linguistic symbol? Why should a pointing gesture not be considered an optional component of a demonstrative's linguistic form? (Langacker, 2008: 250)

Note, however, that Langacker's theoretical statement and the baseball example differ from each other in one important aspect. In the case of the umpire signal, the gesture is a pragmatically mandatory component of the sign. The signal is not performed adequately if one only yells 'Safe!' and does not gesture. Completeness is determined by sports convention; performing the gesture without yelling 'Safe!' is not semantically uninterpretable but is treated as pragmatically unacceptable in this particular context. This is because at some point in time people have agreed on the convention that, in order for the umpire signal to be effective and consequential, the verbal and gestural parts have to be performed together. If this convention is not known to particular language users, their constructicon simply does not involve an entry for this particular multimodal construction, but the unimodal (verbal) construction would most likely be perfectly acceptable for them.[4] Nonetheless, Langacker's umpire example appears to be rather straightforward, and acceptable as an example for a multimodal construction for most Construction Grammarians as both kinesic and verbal parts are presented as forming one unit, in which both parts are obligatory components (presumably also involving a particular prosodic pattern).

However, the theoretical statement Langacker makes in 2001 is more encompassing and, therefore, further reaching. He argues for a conception of language and unit formation as not being restricted to verbal language *in a principled way*. The question that remains unanswered is how the criterion of 'recurrent commonality' can be operationalised. This issue has been of core interest to CxG for quite some time, but it becomes even more eminent once we bring in the full variance of multimodal communication (see Section 4.1 for a detailed discussion). It is grounded, among others, in Goldberg's definition of constructions as frequency dependent:

> Any linguistic pattern is recognized as a construction as long as some aspect of its form or function is not strictly predictable from its components parts or

---

[4] This mirrors the well-known polysemy of the term *constructions*, which refers to both the entrenched units in the minds of individual speakers and the socially shared conventions of a speech community (Tomasello, 2003).

from other constructions recognized to exist. In addition, patterns are stored as constructions even if they are fully predictable *as long as they occur with sufficient frequency.* (Goldberg, 2006: 5, my emphasis)

Innumerable studies have since studied the effects of frequency on unit formation and entrenchment (Bybee, 2006; Schmid, 2007, 2014; Blumenthal-Dramé, 2012; Divjak & Caldwell-Harris, 2015; Divjak, 2019), providing arguments for the unit status of highly frequent instantiations alongside more abstract and/or unpredictable constructional patterns. What unites them is that although frequency of use is indeed considered a core factor for (gradual) entrenchment, they agree on the fact that 'sufficient frequency' is too vague a term and therefore not an operational criterion (Traugott & Trousdale, 2013: 11). At the same time, the exemplar view advocated by Bybee (2010) holds that even constructions that one comes across only once or a couple of times in one's life can be stored in long-term memory if there is some salient aspect to them that makes them stick in the mind. The exact role of frequency in CxG is hence still disputed (Hoffmann, 2013; Ungererer & Hartmann, 2023), and this has implications for multimodal CxG. Most notably, it is impossible to define a frequency threshold for gesture recurrence that any claim about a constructional status of a verbal construction–gesture co-occurrence can be safely based on.[5] This has been the most critical issue in multimodal CxG so far. It touches on the recognisable gap between the general acceptance of the claim that language is multimodal and the difficulties in providing proof that a particular construction is multimodal.

However, note that Goldberg's (2019: 7) definition of constructions has also considerably widened its focus over time to potentially include recurrences in what she calls the 'contextual dimension': 'constructions are understood to be emergent clusters of lossy memory traces that are aligned within our high (hyper!) dimensional conceptual space on the basis of shared form, function, and contextual dimensions'. This openness towards the broad spectrum of usage commonalities has stipulated intensified interest in the status of constructions and the place of non-verbal recurrences within the model. In the following, I review different positions that have recently been proposed to account for multimodality in the CxG framework.

3 Ways to Model the Multimodality of Constructions

Much of the ongoing discussion in multimodal CxG centres around the core issue of what counts as a multimodal construction and how its existence can be proven. Within this discussion, we can identify two main strands and arguments.

---

[5] Here, I use *gesture* in a broad sense as an umbrella term for all meaningful movements of all kinesic articulators.

Quite a few authors (Ningelgen & Auer, 2017; Ziem, 2017; Verhagen, 2021) have advocated the position that constructions are multimodal if and only if a non-verbal component is mandatory – that is, it cannot be omitted without the construction being incomplete on syntactic and/or semantic-pragmatic grounds. This criterion is met by some deictic constructions, which are therefore often discussed as candidate multimodal constructions (Stukenbrock, 2010, 2015, 2021; Ningelgen & Auer, 2017; Balantani, 2022). A case in point are deictic constructions involving [like that/this] or [this ADJ] (German 'so', cf. Ningelgen & Auer, 2017). They are grammatically incomplete and uninterpretable without a gesture that specifies the deictic slot, for example, by depicting how a certain action must be performed ('you need to hold your hand like this') or by specifying the shape of an object or some spatial dimension ('the hole was this big'). For constructions that involve an obligatory gestural component, the multimodal unit status is in fact uncontroversial, even among Construction Grammarians or Interactional Linguists, who nonetheless hold a less restricted view on the nature of multimodal constructionhood.

Figure 2 represents this view on multimodal constructions in terms of obligatory features. The figure is based on the well-known representation of constructions' structure from Croft (2001: 18), which has become the standard representation in usage-based versions of CxG (see also Lehmann 2024 for adaptations to account for multimodal constructions). In contrast to monomodal verbal constructions, the form pole not only consists of syntactic, morphological, and phonological properties, but also involves kinesic properties. Arguably, this is

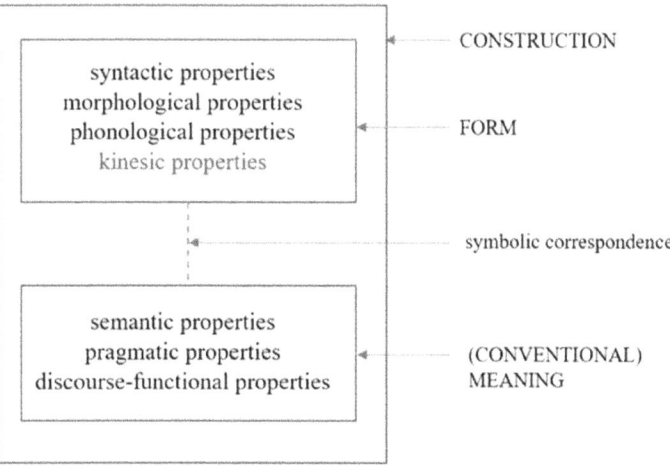

Figure 2 Representation of a multimodal construction with kinesic properties being part of the formal pole (based on Croft, 2001).

a good representation of multimodal constructions that involve obligatory kinesic parts, such as German deictic *so*-constructions.

Consequently, in this view, all multimodal utterances that involve verbal recurrences that are, however, *not grammatically obligatory*, are not considered to instantiate real multimodal constructions. Instead, they are taken to rely on a compositional ad hoc process of combining verbal and kinesic symbols to express a given idea. Hence, two unimodal constructions are combined to form a multimodal construct (or a multimodal composite utterance, Enfield 2009). This process is illustrated by the graphical representation in Figure 3.

The discussion could end here, but I would like to argue, along with some colleagues, that it should not, because otherwise the fundamental questions for CxG raised by the inherent multimodality of language use will remain unresolved. Most importantly, it seems only logical that a usage-based model such as CxG should be able to account for the remarkable consistency in verbo-gestural utterance formation that has been observed in language use. This position has also been entertained recently by Ungerer and Hartmann (2023: 47), who argue that 'if we take the idea seriously that language is a highly dynamic system and that our knowledge of constructions is vast and redundant, rather than limited and highly economic, it makes sense to assume that knowledge about typically co-occurring co-speech gestures or non-verbal elements can form part of a language user's knowledge of a construction'. Nevertheless, it is not an obvious solution to treat all forms of multimodal recurrences, no matter how prevalent they are in usage data, as indexing a multimodal construction of the kind displayed in Figure 1. To tackle this issue, several recent studies have raised the question of the level of granularity at which one assumes a construction to be situated.

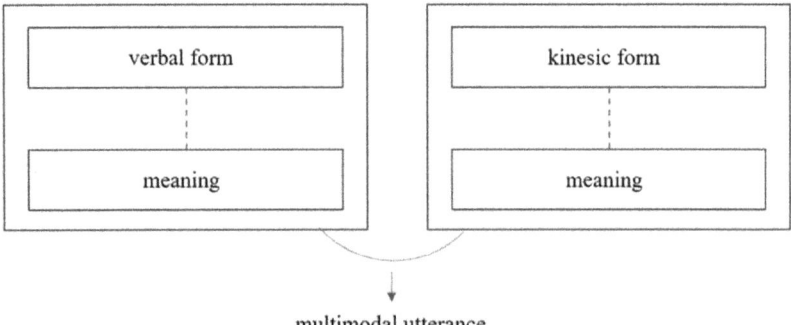

Figure 3 Combination of two monomodal constructions in usage where they form a multimodal utterance (based on Feyaerts et al., 2014).

It is well known that (monomodal) CxGs posit that constructions exist at every level of granularity or schematicity, ranging from highly abstract patterns to lexically and syntactically fully fixed ones ('it's construction all the way down', Goldberg, 2003: 223). They also allow constructions to have optional slots. Lanwer (2017) takes this fundamental premise to argue that it may be arbitrary to posit that verbal elements can be optional but gestural ones need to be obligatory. At the same time, he raises the question of whether non-obligatory elements in verbally defined constructions are cognitively real or whether they rather point towards the existence of different constructions at different levels of granularity. In that vein, Lanwer (2017) suggests that the difference between monomodal and multimodal constructions may be a degree of schematicity. Therefore, for instance, a given multimodal construction that comprises a verbal form that is symbolically linked to a co-speech gesture may be stored alongside the monomodal, verbal format that does not involve a slot for a co-speech gesture. This argument is grounded in the very basic claim of CxG that constructions may be stored redundantly at different levels of granularity. One may, however, wonder about the relations between these two constructions since it is not entirely clear whether the monomodal or the multimodal construction serves as parent construction to the other, whether they are sister constructions, or whether there are no inheritance links altogether.

Accordingly, Lanwer argues that to account for the varying frequencies of constructions' co-occurrence with gestures and the varying degree of the constructions' dependence on gesture, we should consider thinking of a multimodal network of interrelated constructions as prototypically structured and involving fuzzy boundaries. This line of argument is developed further in Uhrig (2022), who has proposed an innovative approach to overcome the discussion on obligatoriness versus optionality of kinesic aspects. He aligns with Ningelgen and Auer (2017) and others in stating that truly multimodal construction, such as that depicted in Figure 1, may be rare. However, instead of dismissing the topic on the grounds that 'real' multimodal constructions are just a tiny and negligible niche within the network, he suggests that knowledge about the combination of verbal and non-verbal signs can be stored as cross-modal associations of varying strength, depending on the strength of statistical association between them. This association is tantamount to the degree of cross-modal collostructional strength as calculated by means of a collostruction analysis (Stefanowitsch & Gries, 2003).[6] Figure 4 represents Uhrig's (2021a) idea of cross-modal associations between monomodal constructions.

---

[6] Uhrig's definition of collstructions slightly differs from the definition of Stefanowitsch and Gries (2003). He defines them broadly as 'the combination of two arbitrary constructions on arbitrary

Figure 4 Representation for the cross-modal association between unimodal constructions (based on Uhrig, 2021a).

Collostructional strength is first and foremost a statistical measure based on the calculation of how often a given verbal construction co-occurs with and without a given gesture and how often that gesture co-occurs with any other construction in a corpus (see also Section 7 for more details). This results in a value that is taken to indicate the strength of association between the construction and the gesture (or any other verbal, para-verbal or non-verbal aspect it may co-occur with). But Uhrig goes further than that, claiming that the strength of association between verbal and non-verbal signs – that is, the cross-modal association – is a statistical measure that is not only dependent on frequency, but it also hinges on the cross-modal semantic-pragmatic interconnectedness. Take, for example, 'yes', which is frequently co-produced with a nod and both the verbal token and the nod can be argued to be co-expressive when paired with each other. However, both the nod and the 'yes' can be produced without one another, and nods also pair with a wide range of other constructions. Therefore, in his view, they are cross-modally associated with each other rather than forming one multimodal form–meaning pairing. Consequently, Uhrig argues that constructions may be situated on a 'cline of co-occurring items', depending on their degree of quantitative and semantic-pragmatic in(ter)dependence.

This view differs from Ziem (2017) and Ningelgen and Auer (2017) in situating knowledge on multimodal usage within the links between constructions rather than the constructions themselves.[7] This position is also entertained by Lehmann (2024), who argues that the incorporation of all information into constructions leads to what Hilpert (2021: 72) has termed the 'fat node' problem: 'current models of the constructional network store nearly all the information in the nodes, while only very little information resides in the connections'. In other words, if the constructions contain all the information that enables their correct use and if the constructions are partly redundantly

---

levels of representation that occur significantly more frequently together than expected' (Uhrig, 2021a).

[7] It is, however, not incompatible with the strict obligatoriness approach since also Uhrig considers truly multimodal construction to be the exception in the system rather than the rule.

stored at different levels of schematicity, the amount of stored information in the constructions – that is, the nodes – will become bigger and bigger, while the network connecting these constructions will be rather weak in comparison. This is argued to be cognitively implausible since it leads to 'rampant redundancy' (Cuyckens & Zawada, 2001: xvii).

Cienki discusses a yet very different idea. He introduces the notion of Utterance Construction Grammar, with utterance defined as 'a level of description above that of speech and gesture for characterizing audio-visual communicative constructions' (Cienki, 2017: 1). The suggestion of (yet) another model of linguistic knowledge is grounded in the conviction that it may be futile to try to coerce gestures into a verbally based constructional framework. By taking the utterance as point of departure, Cienki aligns with Kendon's approach to gesture as 'utterance dedicated visible bodily action' and speech as 'utterance dedicated audible bodily action' (Kendon, 2015: 44, cited in Cienki, 2017: 3) as well as Langacker's concept of the usage event defined as including 'the full phonetic detail of an utterance, as well as any other kinds of signals, such as gestures and body language' (Langacker, 2008: 457, cited in Cienki, 2017: 3). He proposes that constructions have a deep structure as well as a surface structure. These concepts are reminiscent of concepts that are traditionally associated with Generative Grammar, but Cienki stresses that the terms are borrowed without adhering to the nativist assumptions that underlie the Universal Grammar approach. The deep structure is conceptualized as 'a set of tools that can be drawn upon to express the construction', while the surface structure is 'a metonymic representation of some (if not all) elements of the construction' (Cienki, 2017: 3). Consequently, information about gestures that go with a construction is stored in the construction's deep structure. Constructions, in this view, thus exhibit an inherent potential for multimodal realisation, and some aspects of this potential may get activated and visible on the surface representation of a construction – that is, in a construct. Crucially, potential component elements as part of the deep structure may differ in being more or less prototypically associated with the construction. This way of thinking about constructions, Cienki (2017: 5) argues, 'is a more flexible alternative than positing that the model has the binary choice between required and optional elements' and is more compatible with the idea of various degrees of entrenchment. He thus proposes a new way of thinking about many issues that have turned out to be challenging for multimodal CxG. However, in order to book real progress, construction grammarians need to think of ways of putting these ideas to the test.

The discussion on which representation is accurate for which cases and, above all, how we can know for sure is not settled, and I must deceive readers who hope for it to be ultimately resolved here. However, recent years have seen a gradual diversification of approaches and the proliferation of more and more sophisticated methods to conduct research in multimodal CxG. In the following, I review the state-of-the-art research in the field and start with studies that in some way rely on frequency counts to argue for or against the multimodality of a given construction.

4 Studies in Multimodal Construction Grammar

4.1 Frequency-Based Approaches

As outlined previously in this Element, one of the main arguments brought forward in favour of a multimodal reconceptualisation of the constructicon and constructions is grounded in claims that 'any recurrent aspect of a construction's usage can become entrenched' (Langacker 2001). Over the past decade, several studies have shown that manual gestures recurrently and systematically co-occur with given verbal constructions, but co-occurrence frequencies vary strongly. They range from up to 85 per cent for English motion and distance constructions ([all the way from X PREP Y]; see Zima (2014, 2017a, 2017b), and also Pagán Cánovas & Valenzuela (2017)) to approximately 70 per cent for different types of English time expressions (Pagán Cánovas et al., 2020), 58 per cent for English aspectual verbs (Hinell, 2018), 54 per cent on average for English verbs that denote throwing actions (Uhrig, 2022), and 37 per cent (and less) for German modal particles (Schoonjans, 2018). To date, except for Ningelgen and Auer (2017) on deictic *so* ('like this') in German (see the discussion of mandatory gestures with particular deictic expressions earlier in this Element), no study so far reports co-occurrence rates of 100 per cent. Ziem (2017) considers this to be a strong counterargument against the multimodal conception of constructions and the constructicon. Similarly to the line of argumentation of Ningelgen and Auer, he proposes to perform deletion tests, arguing that the input to the meaning of the construction must be so crucial that without the gesture – that is, its deletion – the construction collapses and becomes uninterpretable. If one adopts this definition, it follows that multimodal CxG is nothing more than just a niche within the CxG framework, as there may indeed only be very few verbal constructions that survive the deletion test. But one may wonder whether, from a usage-centred perspective, the more relevant question may not be 'Can it be deleted?' but rather 'Why do speakers use it?'.

In this vein, Hoffmann (2017) emphasises the need for larger-scale data studies and the application of quantitative and statistical methods that go beyond absolute and relative frequencies (as e.g. in Zima, 2014 2017a, 2017b; Schoonjans, 2018). An example of such a quantitative approach is a recent study by Debras on French *je (ne) sais pas* ('I don't know'). Her approach is not explicitly situated within multimodal CxG. However, her paper involves an interesting discussion on why the constructional approach does not do full justice to the semantic-pragmatic import of co-speech gestures, arguing that the original CxG focus on verbal constructions is responsible for the fact that gestures are often regarded as 'secondary and dependant on speech' (Debras, 2021: 42). At the same time, she concludes that the association of the various uses of *je (ne) sais pas* as a pragmatic marker with recurrent gestures is too loose to allow for a straightforward categorisation as a multimodal construction. In this sense, the methodology applied in her study is especially interesting and points to a potentially fruitful direction. Based on a qualitative multimodal analysis of eighty-four occurrences, she first identified three multimodal profiles of *je (ne) sais pas*.[8] A multiple correspondence analysis (e.g., Desagulier, 2017) is then performed to identify the strength of association between all annotated parameters, which include phonetic realisation, prosodic details, functions, type of co-speech gestures, and a couple more. It turns out that the variable 'type of a co-speech gesture' accounts for a large part of the variance in the dataset and is therefore only loosely associated with particular phonetic realisations and functions of *je (ne) sais pas*. Debras therefore concludes that 'combinations of pragmatic markers and recurrent gestures are best described as patterns of contextual configurations in which diverse semiotic resources are assembled into locally relevant multimodal packages' (Debras 2021: 42). Mirroring the ongoing discussion on obligatoriness and frequency in the field of multimodal CxG, these results may be interpreted in two ways: either as evidence for *je (ne) sais pas* clearly not being a multimodal construction, or as an argument for the need for a more nuanced model along the lines proposed by Cienki (2017), Lanwer (2017), Zima (2017a, 2017b), Schoonjans (2018), and Uhrig (2022).

Another innovative approach is the study by Lehmann and Pentrel (2023), who focus on the multimodality of three different *ish*-constructions in modern-day English. They use corpus data from the multimodal NewsScape Library of International TelevisionNews and focus on prosodic and kinesic aspects that co-occur with the different constructional variants of *ish*. Their study reveals that bound -*ish* (such as, e.g., in *soonish*) with 'approximate' meaning is longer in duration and higher in pitch, and shows more pitch variability than bound -*ish* with 'properties' meaning (such as *childish*). Free *Ish* is, again, longer in duration and shows more pitch variability. However, in contrast to bound -*ish*, Ish is always prosodically marked. These three ish-constructions are further associated with different sets of kinesic features, including manual gestures,

---

[8] This is of course still a quite low token number. As more and more multimodal corpora become available, one may hope for more case studies that rely on bigger amounts of data.

head movements, wiggle gestures, mouth movements, gaze direction, as well as eyebrow and eye movements. To test the statistical strength of association between the verbal constructions and the various kinesic features, Lehmann and Pentrel fitted a generalised linear mixed-effects model. They found that none of the kinesic features reaches a significant level in the statistical model, while the prosodic features turned out to be construction specific. The authors thus conclude that prosody is tightly linked to constructional status of *ish*(es), while kinesic aspects are optionally used to support the construction's functions (see also Section 6.2 on the modelling of prosodic recurrences in CxG).

Particularly interesting also is Lehmann's (2024) study on 'tell me about it (TMAI)'. She posits that TMAI is a multimodal construction which comprises a fixed verbal part that is linked to a variable but largely obligatory multimodal part, comprising, among other features, a raised eyebrow gesture. To substantiate this claim, she reports on an experiment that demonstrates two key points. First, hearers experience difficulties in interpreting 'Tell me about it' when it is neither sequentially nor multimodally marked as either a request or a stance marker. Second, hearers are considerably dependent on multimodal features to interpret the construction when a sequential context is missing. Furthermore, the greater the number of kinesic features employed, the easier it is for recipients to discern the intended meaning. Lehmann takes this as evidence that the construction involves a schematic slot for non-verbal information as an integral component of the construction.

Another interesting study, although not concerned with multimodality in *face-to-face* interactions, is presented by Schilperoord and Cohn (2022), who analyse multimodal *before-after* constructions, which consist of an obligatory combination of images and text. Prime examples come from advertisements that promise to change a depicted 'before' state of affairs into a more desirable future state. In a similar vein, some authors have looked at internet memes from a multimodal CxG perspective (Dancygier & Vandelanotte, 2017; Bülow et al., 2018), arguing for them to equally constitute multimodal image-text units.

Besides studies that are explicitly embedded in the CxG framework, a constantly growing body of work of interactional studies equally focusses on the pairing of verbal constructions and bodily conduct. Many of these studies also report frequencies of co-occurrence. We review this body of work in Section 5. However, it seems obvious that frequency and statistical association cannot be taken as sole parameters to model the status of kinesic information with respect to constructions and the network of constructions. The focus on frequency of co-occurrence is no doubt in line with the quantitative turn that has affected all areas of CL since the turn of the century (Janda, 2013). However, a focus that is too much on numbers equally comes with a cost: a lack of rigorous qualitative analysis that is prerequisite to answering the question of why in some situations, speakers do instantiate given non-verbal aspects of constructions, whereas in other situations they do not. Section 4.2, therefore, gives centre stage to perspectives on the meaning import of kinesic recurrences.

4.2 Meaning-Centred Approaches

Lanwer (2017), Schoonjans (2017), and most recently Debras (2021), Lehmann (2024), and Lehmann and Pentrel (2023) all argue that mere frequency is rather uninformative, and to book progress in the field, the analytical focus needs to be transferred to how gestures and other kinesic articulators contribute to utterance meaning. Debras (2021) links this to a general complaint that the focus of CxG is too much on form. She argues that if we take the verbal construction and its form as points of departure, we naturally tend to consider the co-occurring gesture as secondary and optional – that is, something we add while we speak but which we could equally well leave out. Our thinking of constructions and the constructicon, however, may be fundamentally different if we depart from the meaning side (cf. also Lasch 2020 and his meaning-centred approach to the German constructicon) and shift focus to how gesture and speech collaborate to express an idea (the idea unit as proposed by Kendon (2004)). This is the line of argumentation followed by, for example, Bressem and Müller (2017), Hoffmann (2017), Mittelberg (2017), Schoonjans (2018), and (partly) Zima (2014b, 2017a, 2017b). Some studies also explicitly link the instantiations of non-verbal and kinesic aspects to particular functions of a construction (Zima, 2017a, 2017b; Debras, 2021; Lehmann & Pentrel, 2023) and speakers' pragmatic intentions (Zima 2017a). Let us consider an example of the construction [all the way from X to Y] from Zima (2014, also 2017a) (see Example 1):

EXAMPLE 1 KNBC 4 *News at Noon*, December 25, 2012 (UCLA Library NewsScape, Steen et al., 2018; see also Zima 2014: 34).

```
Speaker:   the food is delivered frozen each DAY
           all the way from LONG *bea~(1)ch
           to *LAN*(2)caster
           and they are delivered on the SAME days
           so that clients KNOW
           WHEN they are getting their meals
```

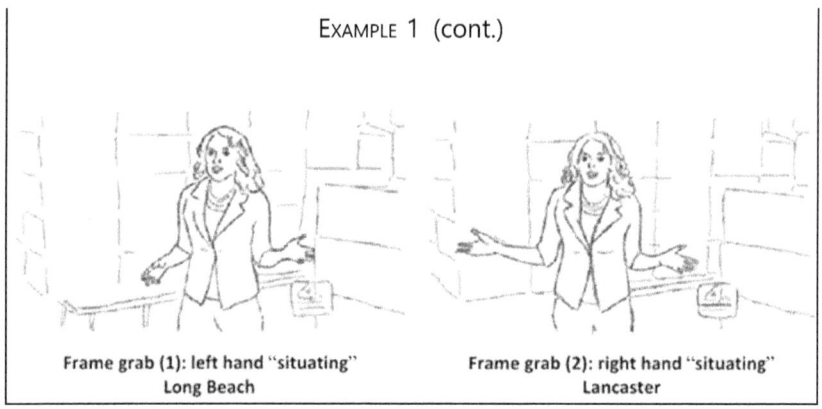

Frame grab (1): left hand "situating" Long Beach

Frame grab (2): right hand "situating" Lancaster

In Example 1, the speaker instantiates a manual gesture that is temporally aligned with the production of the [all the way from X PREP Y]-construction. Frame grab (1) shows the first stroke of the gesture (Kendon 1980) that is co-produced with the articulation of the first geographical reference point (*Long Beach*), which instantiates the X-slot of the constructional template.[9] Frame grab (2) shows the second stroke that is temporally aligned with *Lancaster*. To interpret the gesture, the movement of both hands and their beginning and end points during the holding phases are matched with the co-produced verbal construction so that the right and the left hands are taken to each mark the beginning and end points of the spatial path the speaker refers to. The space between the two extended hands maps on to the distance between the two places.

In the dataset studied in Zima (2014 and 2017a), which comes from various types of English-speaking television broadcasts from the NewScape Library (Steen et al. 2018), 85 percent of the spatial uses of [all the way from X PREP Y] are accompanied by gestures that are formally similar to the gesture the speaker instantiates in Example 1. On the prosodic side, gestural strokes often coincide with prosodic markers, such as focus accents, syllable lengthening, louder voice, and higher pitch. In this example, the speaker further raises her eyebrows while producing the second gestural stroke (cf. Frame grab (2)). All these para- and non-verbal cues are perfectly compatible with the semantics of the verbal construction, which can schematically be described as 'stressing that something is exceptionally big, vast, long, etc.'. If this meaning is already encoded verbally, one may argue that the gesture and the eyebrow movement are *strictu senso* redundant and therefore optional. If one were to perform a deletion test (Ziem, 2017), the manual and facial gesture would therefore probably be considered locally added utterance

---

[9] The stroke phase comprises the movement phase of a manual gesture, during which the gesture unfolds its meaning. It is 'the part people rely on in their interpretation of a gesture' (Bressem & Ladewig, 2011: 54).

components, but not part of the construction. However, speakers always gesture for a reason, and gestures are never meaningless. Following Kendon (2004) and Calbris (2011), they are produced with the *intention* of conveying meaning and therefore cannot be dismissed as 'just optional'. Therefore, instead of treating them as redundant, one may seek to explain their occurrence.

In this and similar examples, the use of verbal, para-verbal, and kinesic aspects to highlight the exceptionality of 'exceptionality' of the path can be attributed to speakers following Givón's (1984) optimality principle: 'more form is more meaning'. By expressing meaning in multiple modalities at once, the proposition of the utterance is emphasised (or profiled in Langackerian terms, Langacker, 1987) – that is, the distance is construed as being exceptionally large. Furthermore, the speaker takes the stance that consequently, the food delivery task is particularly challenging and thus their success in delivering the food each day is applaudable. The construction's semantics, prosody, facial expression, and gesture hence work together to convey semantic and pragmatic meaning. Without the non-verbal cues, these meanings would not be exactly the same. This also holds for Example 2, although in a different way:

EXAMPLE 2 KABC *LIVE WITH REGIS AND KELLY*, APRIL 24, 2007 (UCLA LIBRARY NEWSSCAPE, STEEN ET AL., 2018; SEE ALSO ZIMA 2014: 14).

Kelly Ripa:	mark ROWDE
	and it's a LOT harder than it looks
Michael Strahan:	i- ONE time i tried it with my kids
Kelly Ripa:	hmm
Michael Strahan:	we ended up *going in [CIRc]les for twenty minutes*
	((The circulating gesture is executed for another 4.5 seconds, during which the figure was taken; Strahan pauses his speech during these 4.5 seconds))
Kelly Ripa:	[YES]
	you go in CIRc*les*
	i mean we-
	there was LOTS of near misses with other boots

EXAMPLE 2 (cont.)

In Example 2, the show host Kelly Ripa and her cohost Michael Strahan talk about the difficulties of going straight forward when rowing a boat. Strahan recalls that he once tried to row a boat with his children on board and 'ended up going in circles for twenty minutes'. Starting with 'going', he raises his right arm shoulder level, stretches his index finger, and moves it with the palm open and directed downward, for no less than four and a half seconds, while he is not talking. His words *and* gesture resonate with his interlocutor, Kelly Ripa, who not only copies the verbal construction but also performs the very same gesture (but her arm is held slightly lower, and the gesture is held for a shorter period of time).

From a CxG perspective, Example 2 raises two interesting issues. First, it is obvious that Kelly Ripa interprets the multimodal assembly 'go in circles+manual gesture' as a unit, as she copies it in her own next utterance. She thus interprets the hand gestures as being tightly linked to the [*go in circles*]-constructions although the verbal and the manual part are not neatly aligned with each other on a temporal level in her cohost's utterance.[10] He continues to gesture quite long after the end (of the verbal part) of his turn. Whether this is a local effect or whether both speakers are instantiating a multimodal construction cannot be decided based on this single example (see also Brône & Zima 2015 on ad hoc construction building). However, it seems that, again, the gestures do much more than redundantly encoding information that is already expressed verbally. Rather, they add meaning by depicting and thereby adding details of the movements described. At the same time, verbal semantics, accentuation (focus accent on CIR), and the gestures that are executed in the centre of the interactant's gesture space and held for a considerable stretch of time, serve to highlight the repetitiveness and

---

[10] Zima (2014) found that manual gestures accompany in circles-constructions with a co-occurrence frequency of approximately 60 per cent.

involuntariness of the rowing activity that did not lead them in a particular direction for quite some time. Therefore, both speakers obviously gesture 'with the intent of conveying meaning'. Declaring these speaker-intended meaning aspects as just 'optional' or 'deletable' underemphasises their semantic-pragmatic import. Still, it remains unclear whether the multimodal packages originate from an ad hoc unification process, whether they instantiate a multimodal construction, or whether the recurrences testify to a cross-modal association between the verbal construction and the gesture.

As Uhrig (2022) also observes for verbs denoting acts of throwing, literal uses of 'in circles' are accompanied by a co-verbal manual gesture more often than metaphorical uses (68.75 per cent and 37.14 per cent, respectively, Zima 2014: 21). Although in metaphorical contexts, gestures are less frequent, they still are a recurrent commonality, and, just like with literal uses, add local meaning. This is illustrated in the next example from a CNN news show (see Example 3).

EXAMPLE 3 RED HEN FILE: CNN ELECTION CENTER, JANUARY 5, 2010 (UCLA LIBRARY NEWSSCAPE, STEEN ET AL., 2018; SEE ALSO ZIMA 2014: 15).

```
Bob Kerrey:      HERE is the plan

                 that IS what it's gonna cost

                 here is how we gonna GET there

                 you'll NEver-

                 you'll just be *run*1ni*ng*2 ar*ound*3
                 in *CIR*4cles

                 talking about this forEver
```

In this example, the speaker, Bob Kerrey, uses the [V(motion) in circles]-construction with a metaphorical meaning, referring to ongoing discussions on some political matters. Synchronous to 'running around in circles' he performs a gesture that Ladewig (2011) has termed the 'cyclic gesture': 'it is characterized by a continuous circular movement of the hand, performed away from the body, i.e. outward. The hand remains in place, i.e., it is not moved forwards or sidewards during the performance of the circular motion. ... The movement is perceived as a holistic gestalt as the individual circles are not accentuated at the lower trunk and therefore are not observed as discrete motions' (Ladewig, 2011: 1). In Example 3, the cyclic gesture co-expresses the speaker's stance on the nature of the talks that he argues to be non-productive. At the same time, it serves to disambiguate the meaning of the verbal affiliate construction by not depicting an actual circular movement of the people referred to by the generic 'you' but instead performing a cyclic gesture. This mapping between talking and running in circles, in this example, seems to be licenced by the conceptual metaphors NON-PROGRESS IS NON-FORWARD MOTION (see Kövesces 2010 on the positive correlate PROGRESS IS MOTION FORWARD).

Comparing these two examples of the [V(motion) in circles]-construction, they illustrate that although they share a semantic core meaning, there is considerable formal variance in the manual gestures performed by the speakers (for more details, see Zima 2014 and 2017b). In addition, there is variance with respect to the temporal relationship between the gesture(s) and the lexical affiliates with which they are partly co-expressive. As Schoonjans (2017) discusses in more detail, this is a common feature of gestures, since the performance of gesture phrases and units may take more time than the articulation of the lexical affiliate. Moreover, the lexical affiliate may not be just one verbal construction but a larger semantic unit within an utterance. However, variance is an intrinsic feature of language use tout court, even if one restricts the focus on the verbal channel only. Therefore, variance in use is an issue that CxG needs to deal with even if multimodality is left out of the picture.[11]

---

[11] Crucially, the intra- and interindividual differences at all levels of language production concern not only the dimension of (multimodal) language use but also the level of individual language users' linguistic knowledge, as stressed by Ungerer and Hartmann (2023: 50):

> If we conceive of CxG as a theory of linguistic knowledge, the question arises whose linguistic knowledge it is that we are actually describing. The fact that Construction Grammarians for a long time tended to abstract away from individual differences might be a bit surprising at first glance, as the declared goal of the paradigm is 'to find out what speakers know when they know a language and to describe this knowledge as accurately as possible' (Hilpert 2013: 1–2). From this perspective, it is crucial to take the level of the individual into account, especially given the mounting evidence that speakers differ significantly in their linguistic knowledge (e.g. Dąbrowska 2012).

However, the widening of the focus to include all semiotic channels leads to an exponential increase in this variance, which complicates attempts to pin down the nature of recurrences in observed behaviour. This is also exemplified, among others, in the work of Bressem (2013), Bressem and Müller (2017), and Schoonjans (2018).

Schoonjans' (2018) monograph on German modal particles and the role of manual and head gestures to co-express down-toning meanings is the first book-length treatment of the topic of multimodal CxG. Not only was his study among the very first to raise theoretical questions, but he also presents a large-scale corpus analysis that inquires in detail into the interdependence of verbal constructions and non-verbal co-occurrence patterns. The frequencies reported for multimodal instantiations of the modal particles under scrutiny are rather low (37 per cent and less), but this should not lead one to dismiss Schoonjans' results and approach. Indeed, he raises and discusses several issues which are critical for future endeavours in multimodal CxG. These include the problem that recurrence involves the assumption that there is a stable formal and semantic core that is common to all instantiations and results from subtraction of all in situ variation. However, as Bressem (2013) illustrates, the form of manual gestures can vary in a great number of dimensions, including hand shape, orientation, movement and position in gesture space; therefore, 'no two tokens of gesture are ever identical' (Harrison, 2009: 82). Put differently, the issue of whether two gesture tokens are instantiations of the same gesture type is far from trivial.

This is also illustrated by Bressem and Müller (2017) in their study of the so-called throwing-away gesture. They illustrate that this gesture can be combined with several different verbal constructions, including a wide range of grammatical categories such as particles, nouns, verbs, and adverbs. The throwing-away gesture is 'characterized by a particular kinesic core: a lax flat hand oriented vertically with the palm facing away from the speaker's body flapping downwards from the wrist' (Bressem & Müller, 2017: 3). Just as Mittelberg (2017) argues for palm-up, open-hand gestures that co-occur with German existential constructions, Bressem and Müller argue for an experiential basis of the gesture which they situate in the embodied experience of throwing concrete entities away. This is extended to metaphorical uses when referring to abstract objects in speech. They thus identify a constructional pattern, which they term 'negative assessment construction', with the multimodal form [throwing away gesture] + [particles/negation/N/V/ADV]. From a theoretical perspective, they suggest that whether constructions are multimodal in nature is probably not a polar question requiring a yes or no answer. Rather, verbal constructions may constitute a multimodal network, with some of them being more and others less bound to particular gestures. This is very much in line with Uhrig (2021a, 2021b) and his idea of cross-modal associations that was sketched in Section 3.

In a similar vein, Mittelberg (2017) presents a case study on the German existential construction [*es gibt* X] ('*there is an* X'; see also Hampe et al., 2018 on there-constructions). Departing from an emergent grammar perspective, which takes grammar to be 'the name for certain categories of observed repetitions in discourse' (Hopper, 1998: 156), she argues that the [es gibt]-construction involves a slot for a gestural enactment that depicts an act of 'giving or holding something' (Mittelberg, 2017: 1). This gestural re-enactment is grounded in the basic pattern of experience that Goldberg has argued to motivate (di)transitive constructions: 'the initial meaning is an experiential gestalt. This basic pattern of experience is encoded in a basic pattern of language' (Goldberg, 1998: 208). Consequently, Mittelberg (2017: 2) argues that 'the basic manual actions of giving and holding . . . motivate multimodal instantiations of existential constructions in German discourse'. Drawing on semi-experimental data of German spoken discourse, she illustrates that *es gibt*-constructions co-occur with unimanual variants of the palm-up, open-hand gesture as well as bimanual, palm-vertical, open-hand gestures.[12] Contrary to my arguments concerning formal variance despite a common semantic core for motion constructions (Zima 2014, 2017b), however, her analysis shows formal recurrence in the gestures, while their semantic-pragmatic meaning is clearly situated and dependent on the discursive context. The semantic recurrence only holds for the very schematic meaning of 'holding some kind of imaginary entity'. As Mittelberg acknowledges, her analyses are preliminary, but her work on existential constructions points towards candidate constructions for future research in multimodal CxG by suggesting that 'linguistic constructions that recruit basic embodied manual actions and interactions with the physical and social world are particularly likely to be instantiated multimodally and thus also engender emergent multimodal patterns, or clusters, of experience' (Mittelberg, 2017: 5).

This overview of recent studies with a multimodal constructional perspective illustrates the variety of approaches that have already been pursued in this young field of research (see also the contributions in Nikiforidou and Fried, 2025). As mentioned earlier, the issues of multimodal co-occurrence and unit formation are, however, not discussed only in CxG, but the topic has recently also gained traction in interactional linguistic work. Findings and methods of research are no doubt relevant for the ongoing discussion within CxG. Section 5 thus broadens the perspective to include research that is less concerned with issues of languages as systems but rather focusses on unit formation in and through interaction.

---

[12] Mittelberg's study does not involve information on the frequency of this co-occurrence.

5 Interactional Research on Multimodal Packages

In recent years, a growing number of studies with a conversation-analytic or interactional linguistic background (a.o. Stukenbrock, 2010, 2021; Mondada, 2014; Pekarek Doehler, 2016, 2019, 2022; Keevallik, 2020; Debras, 2021; Balantani, 2022; Pekarek Doehler et al., 2022) has focussed on 'recurrent simultaneous or successive combinations of grammatical constructions and bodily behavior' (Pekarek Doehler, Keevallik, Li, 2022: 1; emphasis in original). Although the names given to these observed patterns of verbal and non-verbal elements vary (*multimodal package*, Hayashi, 2005; Stukenbrock, 2015; Kärkkäinen & Thompson, 2018; *multimodal assembly*, Pekarek Doehler, 2019; *multimodal Gestalt*, Mondada, 2014, 2024; *multimodal profile*, Debras, 2021; *multimodal social action format*, Pekarek Doehler, 2022; *recurrent grammar-position-body constellations*, Pekarek Doehler, 2016; *syntactic-bodily unit*, Keevallik 2020), reflecting slightly different research foci and perspectives, all these studies unite around a common interest in systematically and frequently occurring couplings of verbal and kinesic forms that serve 'to accomplish particular interactional tasks' (Pekarek Doehler et al., 2021: 1). The primary concern of these studies is with the workings of social interaction and how people achieve to do things together in interaction. This is very much in line with the traditional focus of CA on observable, everyday activities (Sacks, 1992) and its surface-orientated method to analyse conversational data. Through the method of sequential analysis, researchers aim to reconstruct the methods of making sense of the interaction (cf. Zima, Auer & Rühlemann, 2025). Most importantly, researchers aim to 'ground their analysis in how the participants themselves respond to and interpret interactional phenomena in their subsequent reactions' (Deppermann, 2012: 747). This imperative to stay as close to the data as possible and to reconstruct the interactants' actions in their reciprocity and interconnectedness leads some to take a more or less openly anti-cognitivist view, rejecting all reference to cognitions as pure speculation about non-observable processes within the interactants' minds (see in detail Imo, 2011). Although this view has been called into question by a number of pioneering figures in the field (Imo, 2011; Deppermann, 2012), only very few authors (Stukenbrock, 2010; Debras, 2021) raise the question whether the patterns they identify in interactional data – that is, in language usage data – qualify as multimodal constructions of individuals and/or the speech community. Given the broader aim to describe recurrent, routinised patterns, CA- and IL-informed studies may, however, still turn out to be fruitful starting points for investigations in multimodal CxG.

Just like Ningelgen and Auer (2017), Stukenbrock (2010, 2021) studies German deictic *so* (like this)-constructions and shows that the verbal part is only complete and interpretable if accompanied by a manual action of depiction. This concerns uses of *so* together with an adjective *(so groß*, this big), a verb *(so schwimmen*, swimming like this), *so* followed by a performance indicating that one needs to do something as depicted *(du must das so machen*, you have to do it like this), and *so* as used in the constructional template 'so sieht/sehen X aus' (X look(s) like that). In a similar vein, studying music rehearsal, Balantani (2022) argues that non-lexical vocalisations pair with try-marked German *so_was* (something like this) to form a multimodal package in establishing joint decisions. Both studies thus testify to the observation that in German *so*-constructions, the kinesic, non-verbal depictions are integral parts of the multimodal gestalt introduced by *so* (and *so_was*). Therefore, Stukenbrock (2021: 4) argues, '[So-constructions] are prime candidates to argue for multimodal constructions not as locally routinized phenomena, but as sedimented multimodal constructions. They have grammaticalized the context-bound conditions of their use – this includes, first and foremost, embodied practices (Bühler, 1934; Stukenbrock, 2015) to establish joint attention (Diessel, 1999, 2006)' (see also Ningelgen & Auer, 2017, who argue along similar lines).

Another verbal construction that has received considerable attention in multimodal CA – a term coined by Mondada (2014) – is French *je ne sais pas* (I don't know). Pekarek Doehler (2016, 2019, 2022) investigates *je ne sais pas* (I don't know) and its phonologically reduced form *chais pas* (dunno), arguing that the full form is used predominantly as a response token indicating a lack of epistemic access or knowledge on the part of the answerer. Most importantly, the full form used in this function is paired with gaze towards the questioner and sometimes also accompanied by a shrug. On the other hand, the reduced form functions as a *pre-beginning* (Schegloff, 1997) element, which projects (Auer, 2005) a dispreferred response or a disaffiliative stance. This use is accompanied by gaze aversion.

These findings are supported by a cross-linguistic study by Pekarek Doehler, Polak-Yitzhaki, Li, Stoenica, Havlíka, and Keevallik (2022) on *I don't know* (IDK)-constructions in Czech, French, Hebrew, Mandarin, and Romanian. Drawing on the analysis of video recordings of spontaneous talk-in-interaction, they argue for the existence of an [IDK + gaze aversion]-pattern, which they describe as serving 'as a routinized multimodal resource for prefacing a dispreferred response: It indexes incipient resistance to the constraints set out or to the stance conveyed by the coparticipant's prior action' (Pekarek Doehler et al., 2021: 3). Most strikingly, they observe gaze aversion to be coupled with IDK used as a preface to a dispreferred response in around 90 per cent of cases for all languages studied. However, as I will show in Section 6.1, the exceptionally high co-occurrence rates cannot be reproduced for German and in data where gaze is not analysed from a third-person person perspective but recorded with mobile eye-tracking glasses. Furthermore, as mentioned earlier, gaze is an omnipresent resource in interaction, as we can refrain from gesturing, but we always gaze someplace while we talk. This, I will argue, makes it harder to reliably relate a given gaze pattern to a particular construction.

Kärkkäinen and Thompson (2018) present a multimodal analysis of English type-confirming yes and no responses to polar questions, showing that in approximately 60 per cent of cases, these responses are realised as multimodal packages – that is, a combination of the response token and postures, manual gestures, and gaze. In a similar vein, Kendrick and Holler (2017) show that dispreferred responses to English polar questions are paired to a statistically significant degree with gaze aversion, while preferred responses are much more likely to be uttered with the answerer's gaze being directed at the questioner. Relating these findings to the work of Pekarek et al. (2021) and their results on turn-initial, responsive *I don't know*, it is, however, unclear whether these gaze patterns are typical of responses to polar questions only or whether gaze aversion is linked to dispreference on a more general level or even answer complexity as dispreferred answers tend to be more complex than preferred ones (Auer & Zima, in preparation). To tackle this question, more research is needed on different turn-initial constructions, types of question, and requests, but also on gaze at turn beginnings in general. I will also elaborate on these issues in Section 6.1, albeit I will not be able to give a fully satisfactory answer as of yet.

Many more studies focus on how verbal constructions are used together with non-verbal conduct to accomplish a given interactional task. However, they present qualitative analyses of selected examples only or focus on multimodal constructs in which a kinesic part completes a syntactically incomplete utterance (Keevallik, 2013). These instances are prime examples of multimodal composite utterances or of local multimodality emerging from the activity at hand. However, they do not necessarily point towards the existence of a multimodal schema. In that vein, Mondada (2014) adds to that body of research by focussing on multimodal gestalts that emerge while walking and talking. She shows how the whole body moves in systematic ways. However, she does not make any claims about cognitive representation or conventionalisation.

All of these studies contribute to our understanding of how verbal and kinesic modalities work together to convey meaning in interaction and to contribute to social actions. Not all of them are immediately relevant to multimodal CxG as they do not concentrate on one single or a couple of interrelated constructions but focus on social actions and how they get accomplished by interactants. Nevertheless, they all testify to the fact that the growing interest in multimodal unit formation does not only concern CxG but is a rising topic in multimodal CA as well. However, the reasons for this interest are very different. While conversation analysts focus on practices of social behaviour in interaction, they are by and large refraining from making claims about the exact nature of the recurrent units and their mental representation.

Furthermore, some studies raise the question whether recurrences of all semiotic modalities are equally indicative of multimodal unit formation. To elucidate this issue, Section 6 will shift the perspective beyond manual gestures. I will first focus on gaze and its multifaceted role in interaction, which makes it difficult to link a given gaze pattern to a particular construction (Section 6.1). In Section 6.2, we address the role of prosody as part of multimodal constructions and the question of whether unimodal prosodic constructions exist.

6 Beyond Gestures: Gaze and Prosody

6.1 Competing Motivations for Gaze Patterns

The role of gaze in social interaction has received scholarly attention in CA from very early on, with research on the turn-regulative functions of gaze dating back to the 1960s and 1970s (Kendon, 1967; Argyle & Cook, 1976; Goodwin, 1980). The multimodal turn in CA has reignited this interest, and a growing number of recent studies have paid attention to gaze, either in passing or as an explicit research topic. Accordingly, a few recent studies from CA and IL backgrounds have proposed a given gaze behaviour to par with verbal constructions in forming multimodal units (Ningelgen & Auer, 2017; Pekarek Dohler et al., 2021; Pekarek Doehler, 2022).

For instance, as outlined in Section 5, studies on 'I don't know' (IDK)-constructions in French, Romanian, Mandarin, Hebrew, and Czech (Pekarek Doehler et al., 2022) argue that in interaction, 'I don't know' (or phonologically reduced forms such as French *chais pas*) is accompanied by gaze aversion if used as a preface to a disaffiliative response. This corroborates previous claims that gaze aversion in responsive actions signals and even projects disaffiliation (Haddington, 2006; Kidwell, 2006; Bröker & Zima, 2022; Calabria & de Stefani, 2024; Lehmann, forthcoming, but see Laner, 2025, on gaze patterns in assessments in mobile interaction). It ties in with Kendrick and Holler's (2017) findings on gaze aversion accompanying dispreferred responses to polar questions, although disaffiliation and dispreference are distinct phenomena. Whereas affiliation is defined as the actions through which 'the hearer displays support of and endorses the teller's [or interactant's, E. Z.] conveyed stance' (Stivers, 2008: 35), disaffiliative actions express divergence and disagreement. Therefore, affiliation affects the negotiation of the relationship between the interactants on a social level. Preference, in turn, is a more complex issue as one may distinguish responses that are grammatically preferred (e.g. interjection answers such as 'yes' or 'no' which match the question's polarity ('You don't like tea?' 'No.') or repetition-type answers as in 'You won't come to the party, do you?' 'No, I won't') from pragmatically or socially preferred ones, such as accepting an apology or an invitation. The findings of Kendrick and Holler (2017: 15–16) are based on grammatical preference only, and not all their examples of grammatically dispreferred responses are disaffiliative.

While the details on the role of gaze in responsive actions may be of minor importance to the topics that are central for multimodal CxG, I believe that more general issues concerning the analysis of gaze within multimodal packages and multimodal constructions are worthwhile to discuss in more detail. To this aim, I briefly report results of a small-scale case study on responsive *Ich weiß nicht* (I don't know) and phonologically reduced *weiß nich(t)* (dunno) in German interactions. It is based on fifty-five examples of the full and phonologically reduced forms of *ich weiß nicht*. They were extracted from seventeen hours of dyadic and triadic interactions in which participants were sitting around a coffee table while their gaze behaviour was recorded with mobile eye-tracking glasses (cf. Figure 5 and Figure 6 for exemplar screenshots from the data[13]).

As a first step, we only analysed instantiations of *ich weiß nicht* that were produced in turn-initial position, as part of a responsive actions, and which were not followed by a complement clause (*ich weiß nicht, ob* ... / I don't know if ...). Thirty-five instances that met these selection criteria were epistemic uses. They indicated a lack of knowledge on the part of the respondent and therefore an inability to respond appropriately and to comply with the intent to receive information. Twenty examples constitute prefaces to a disaffiliative stance, such as, for example, *I don't know, I don't really like being around too many people*. Epistemic uses were accompanied by gaze aversion in 46 per cent of the cases, while 75 per cent of speakers who produced *(ich) weiß nich(t)* as a preface to a disaffiliative stance averted their gaze from their interlocutor(s). The absolute numbers are, of course, very low and the results need to be supported by further research, but the numbers point to a significant difference ($X^2 = 4,4381$; df = 1, p = 0.035) in gaze behaviour between the two uses of *(ich) weiß nich(t)*.

---

[13] Coloured circles in the first-perspective video recording indicate the visual focus of the person wearing the eye-tracking glasses. For analysis, the recordings of the eye-tracking glasses and the of the external camera are synchronised and arranged in a split screen video. In Figure 6, the recordings of the study participants' glasses are arranged to match the seating arrangement of the participants. Accordingly, the recording of the person on the left is shown in the bottom left of the split-screen video. Above, you see the recording of the person sitting in the middle, and the recording of the glasses of the person on the right corresponds to the video displayed on the upper right side of the split screen.

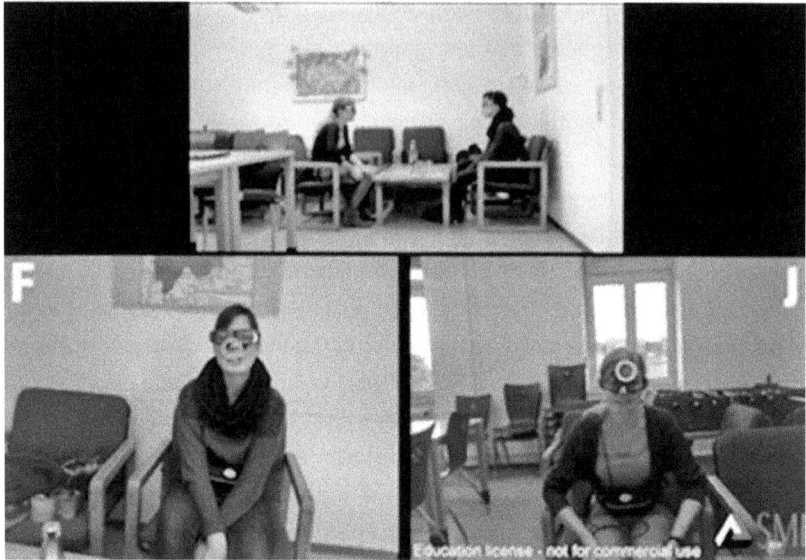

Figure 5 Screenshot of dyadic recording (with SMI eye-tracking glasses).

Figure 6 Screenshot of a triadic recording (with Tobii Glasses 2).

To allow for comparison with previous research on the multimodality of IDK-constructions and most notably Pekarek Doehler et al. (2021), we further restricted the dataset to instances in which the construction did not constitute one turn constructional unit (TCU) of its own but was prosodically integrated in a larger TCU. Furthermore, *(ich) weiß nich(t)* had to be produced as a dispreferred response to questions, assessments, proposals, and informings.

This left us with thirty-seven instantiations, only in 59.5 percent of which the speakers averted their gaze from their interlocutor(s). This is significantly less gaze aversion than the 90.8 percent (on average) reported by Pekarek Doehler et al. (2021).

There may be several reasons for the difference in numbers. One of them is the fact that we used mobile eye tracking to record participants' gaze behaviour whereas Pekarek Doehler and colleagues analysed gaze in interactions that were recorded from the perspective of the observer. A recent experimental study (Zima, Auer & Rühlemann, 2025) has shown that an accurate description of gaze is highly dependent on the availability of eye-tracking information. I will briefly elaborate on that methodological issue in Section 7, but more importantly, the claim on whether we are really dealing with a multimodal package or even a multimodal construction hinges on the question of whether the observed gaze behaviour is locally linked to the meaning of the verbal construction or whether the co-occurrence is due to other constraints, such as the very fact that answerers utter *I don't know* at turn beginnings and avert their gaze because they need to plan their next utterance. It has been repeatedly argued that utterance planning is facilitated by gaze aversion because the reduction of visual input reduces the speaker's cognitive load (Beattie, 1979; Glenberg et al., 1998), making more resources available for utterance planning. It follows that if the average frequency of gaze aversion with turn-initial *(ich) weiß nich(t)* and the frequency of gaze aversion at turn beginnings in general do not differ from each other in a statistically significant way, there are no strong arguments for the claim that gaze aversion is part of a multimodal package.

Despite claims that speakers avoid looking at their interlocutors when planning the next turn, which date back to Kendon (1967), exact frequency counts for turn aversion at turn beginnings are scarce. For example, Ho et al. (2015) investigated gaze aversion at the beginning of the turn and, through cross-recurrence analysis, confirmed that gaze aversion precedes the beginnings. Unfortunately, however, no concrete information is given on how often the speakers actually gaze away at the very beginning of their turns. To close that gap, we annotated a randomly collected selection of 120 turn transitions from our eye-tracking data for gaze aversion in the time interval of 500 milliseconds before and after turn onset. The results are plotted in Figure 7. It shows that on average speakers avert their gaze at turn beginning in 57.7 per cent of cases. These numbers are based on a very small dataset and are no doubt preliminary. Also, an ongoing project on gaze aversion in question-answer sequences in English and German triadic interaction (Auer & Zima, in preparation) suggests that with roughly 65 per cent, gaze aversion at turn beginnings is slightly more frequent in responses to questions than in the very broad and diverse umbrella

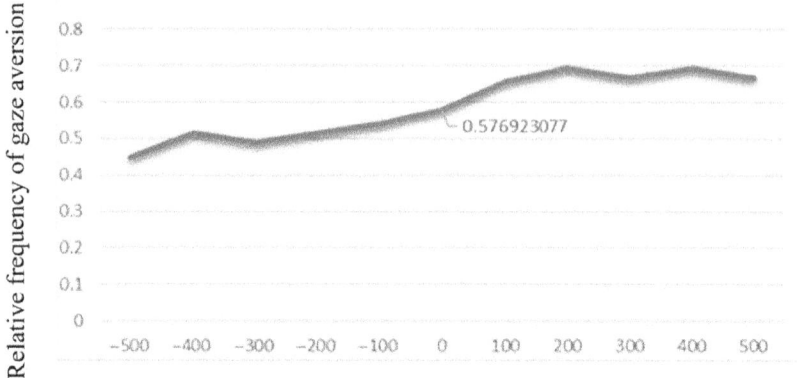

Milliseconds before and after the onset of the turn (=0)
(negative values: time before onset; positive values: after onset;
coding in 100-millisecond intervals)

Figure 7 Graph showing the average relative frequency of speaker gaze aversion before, at the beginning, and shortly after the beginnings of turns.

category of 'turn transitions', which covers all kinds of sequential position, turn lengths, etcetera.[14]

Nevertheless, the analyses illustrate an important issue: any claim on gaze playing a fundamental role for the multimodality of *ich weiß nicht*-constructions crucially hinges on a significantly higher frequency for gaze aversion for turn-initial *ich weiß nicht* compared to gaze aversion at turn beginnings or in responsive actions in general. If the preliminary frequencies for German *ich weiß nicht* (59.5 per cent) and for gaze aversion at turn transitions (57.7 per cent) were confirmed on larger datasets, this claim would not be tenable, as the difference in frequency is statistically not significant.

This does not entail that a given gaze behaviour cannot be part of a multimodal construction per se. For example, Ningelgen and Auer (2017) argue that German deictic 'so' construction requires speaker and recipient gaze to be directed at the manual action that fills the slot that is opened by 'so' (like this). However, given the higher-order functions that gaze fulfils in interaction, among which are managing turn-taking, monitoring interlocutors, displaying attention and engagement, etcetera, one needs to probably be particularly cautious in claiming a given gaze behaviour to be part of a multimodal package or a particular construction. Most importantly, these higher-order functions are not semantically linked to the proposition of the utterance but ensure the

---

[14] Most notably, gaze aversion seems to be linked to the structural complexity of the planned answer.

progressivity of interactions. This is, of course, not to say that gaze cannot fulfil lower-order functions, such as pointing, in which cases a semantic relationship with the co-produced constructions may exist. But in general, gaze behaviour may be harder to link to a given construction than is the case for, for example, manual or head gestures and alternative explanations need to be considered. After this brief excursion into the functions of gaze in interaction, Section 6.2 pays special attention to prosody and its role in CxG.

6.2 Prosody as Part of Constructions and Prosodic Constructions

Prosody is often referred to as the para-verbal modality, alongside verbal language and non-verbal, kinesic behaviour. Although prosody is thus treated as being situated outside language proper, the term suggests a closer alliance with language than is generally ascribed to the non-verbal modalities. This seems justified, since it is possible, at least in principle, not to gesture, whereas spoken language is necessarily produced with some kind of intonation contour, stress pattern, pitch, etcetera. Therefore, the connection between prosody and grammatical constructions seems more immanent than with gestures (and gaze). Nevertheless, both the questions of whether prosodic features are intrinsic parts of constructions, and whether the constructicon includes monomodal, prosodic constructions are equally controversially discussed, as is the case for kinesic recurrences. However, Interactional Linguists often take a more cautious stance on this issue, while Construction Grammarians seem to have fewer concerns.

This is illustrated, for instance, in the contributions in a recent collective volume (in German), edited by interactional linguists Wolfgang Imo and Jens Lanwer (2020). While the editors stress in their editorial that CxG is uniquely positioned to account for possible routinised and conventionalised prosodic patterns that pair with verbal constructions, many of the studies in the volume conclude that prosodic features are better described as contextualisation cues (Gumperz, 1982, 1992) than features of the constructions themselves.[15] This is grounded in the observation that there is so much variation in the various dimensions of prosodic production of utterances that one would have to assume an unreasonably high number of distinct constructions, leading to a tremendous increase in stored units and hence of redundancy in the constructicon.

For example, Droste and Günthner (2020) study syntactically disintegrated German 'du' (*you*)-formats that are used in affiliative contexts; not only as shifters

---

[15] Contextualisation cues are verbal, para-verbal, or non-verbal signals that guide the recipient in drawing inferences to interpret contextualized utterances. They are 'any feature of linguistic form that contributes to the signalling of contextual presuppositions' (Gumperz, 1982: 131).

(Silverstein 1976) to induce contact with a recipient but in positions in which it indexes both 'a break with what has immediately preceded and the necessity of local reorientation' (Droste & Günthner, 2021: 91). Drawing on a wide range of data of spontaneous multiparty interactions in German, they show that disintegrated 'du' realises interrelated functions which correlate with particular prosodic features and sequential positions. Most importantly, they show that 'du' is treated by interactants as indexing a larger break in the interaction the more it is prosodically marked and the less it is integrated into the utterance. Therefore, the authors argue, prosody acts as an almost prototypical contextualisation cue that guides interactants in the interpretation of the ongoing activity. To claim constructional status for all pairings of one, sequential position, two, its prosodic integration, which is a continuous rather than a binary category, and three, its interactional functions, would lead to rampant growth of the constructional network. Even more fundamentally, the authors argue that this would equate the concept of 'interactional practice' with that of constructions, implying that communication comes down to a compositional process of instantiating constructions, defined as mentally stored, fixed units. However, this view has been rejected repeatedly by interactional linguists such as Deppermann (2011) and Günther (2011), who see constructions as sedimented patterns that interactants do not instantiate one on one but *orient to* and reconfigure flexibly in use to meet local interactional contingencies.

A similar stance is taken by Dagmar Barth-Weingarten, Elizabeth Couper-Kuhlen, and Arnulf Deppermann (2020) in their paper on stand-alone 'oh' in English informal conversations. They present a detailed phonetic and prosodic analysis of 'oh', which includes pitch contours, length, loudness, tempo, and voice quality (and the preceding information to which the recipient reacts). It leads them to conclude that none of these prosodic characteristics correlates with specific functions or sequential positions of 'oh' to an extent that would justify modelling them as part of the construction. Furthermore, they illustrate that the local meaning of 'oh' is so dependent on particular details of the interaction, such as, for instance, the degree of engagement as expressed in empathy displays, that attribution of these details to the constructions would not only worsen CxG's 'fat node problem' (Hilpert 2021), but it would require almost every token to be declared a construction, which, of course, is in conflict with the basic premises of CxG.[16]

However, this analysis is only partly compatible with Reber (2012: 241), who studied English 'sound objects' *ah* and *oh* and claims that they are indeed linked to 'obligatory prosodic-phonetic properties'. Nevertheless, she too does not opt

---

[16] As one of the reviewers rightly pointed out, this would be less problematic in an approach to constructions that considers them to be lossy traces of memory (Goldberg 2019) or exemplary clouds rather than fixed pairings of form and meaning.

for a constructional approach, but argues that the segmental and prosodic channels are better viewed as contextualisation systems.

Barth-Weingarten (2011: 360) takes a more optimistic stance. Studying German *jaja* (yes yes), she shows that *jaja* 'in German talk-in-interaction can be realized in a wide range of prosodic-phonetic variants, which are systematic in so far as they are connected to specific interactional functions and sequential consequences'. She interprets her findings as proof for 'that, at least perhaps with response tokens, certain prosodic-phonetic features may contextualize certain "meanings" across sequence organisation contexts, response tokens and core forms of individual tokens' (362). Nonetheless, her conclusions are rather cautious: 'This then would simplify the memory task and thus their employment by the participants, although we should still be careful to assume a fixed, context-independent 1:1 form–meaning relationship.' Despite this cautious conclusion, Barth-Weingarten's study was one of the first to argue for prosodic features to pair with verbal forms in systematic ways and paved the way for further inquiry.

Some recent studies, therefore, explicitly argue for prosodic aspects to be part of the formal pole of multimodal construction. For instance, Põldvere and Paradis (2020: 307) found that the construction *what-x* (*What she would eat it?*), which is reactive to a preceding turn by another speaker and indicates some problem of understanding, 'forms one tone unit with the complement and never carries a nuclear pitch accent. The core meaning is to signal an immediate reaction to something said by another speaker in the preceding turn, and the dialogic functions include questions proper as well as expressions of disagreement'. Based on their findings, the authors explicitly argue for the need for 'a crucial theoretical extension of Construction Grammar involving a broadening of the concept of construction to cover not only the lexical-semantic pairing but also prosodic properties and the role of the construction in the interactive dialogic space in speech' (307). This argument is supported by Lehmann's (2024: 7) study on stance-related 'Tell me about it' (supra), which she argues qualifies as a 'genuinely multimodal construction, i.e., a construction with both entrenched prosodic and morphosyntactic properties'. Combing qualitative analyses with a forced choice experiment, she shows that stance-related *Tell me about it* is realised with slower tempo than when used as a request – that is, an other-initiation of a storytelling sequence. Most strikingly, language users use prosody as the sole disambiguation cue between the two uses of 'Tell me about it', when no other cues are provided (such as sequential context). Thus, Lehmann seems to rightly conclude that 'this knowledge on the two uses of *Tell me about it* must be stored in the language users' minds in some way' (11).

Lanwer (2017, 2020) takes a similar stance in his work on German appositive structures. He identifies three patterns: First Name-Surname-Appositions (Toni Kroos, Fußballgott; *Toni Kross, God of football*), Role-Name-Appositions (meinen Gast, Peter Sloterdijk; *my guest, Peter Sloterdijk*), and Repair-Appositions (vom Character indelebilis – also vom unauslöschlichen Siegel; *from the character indelibilis, that means from the indelible seal*). His analysis of their prosodic realisations reveals that all three patterns are associated with distinct prosodic features, such as a fixed accent position with Role-Name-Appositions. These, he argues, need to be integrated in the constructional representation.

Mounting evidence for the existence of multimodal constructions as pairings of morphosyntactic and phonetic-prosodic structure also comes from Ogden (2010), who studies prosodic constructions in complaining activities, and a very recent study by Masini et al. (in press). Their focus is on the use of list constructions in spoken Italian. Studying ninety-two naturally occurring instances, they show that first, lists are 'characterized by a lower speech/articulation rate with respect to non-listing speech. Second, non-compositional lists, which require a greater processing effort, are produced slower than more compositional lists. Third, all lists, irrespective of their interpretation, are typically associated with tonal parallelism' (Masini et al., in press: 116). Accordingly, the authors argue that all these prosodic features need to be incorporated into the list constructional network.

Alongside research on prosodic features as part of multimodal constructions, it has been suggested that grammar also includes monomodal prosodic constructions, 'i.e., assemblies of prosodic features that convey a particular meaning (relatively) independent of the words that are used with it' (Lehmann, 2024: 2). For English, Ward (2019) has described a range of what he calls 'prosodic constructions', defined as the pairing of prosodic forms and meanings that are independent and of higher order than the verbal constructions with which they co-occur. One such example is the positive assessment construction which unites a couple of prosodic features such as high pitch, creaky voice, loudness, and long duration. The existence of prosodic constructions has also been described for French (Marandin, 2006), Persian (Sadat-Tehrani, 2010), and Spanish (Gras & Elvira-García, 2021) but since these are not multimodal but unimodal constructions, this body of work is not immediately relevant for the topic of multimodal CxG and will therefore not be outlined in more detail at this point.

In sum, work on the integration of prosodic recurrences into the CxG framework touches upon some of the same issues that were also raised in the context of gestures and, to a lesser degree, gaze: prosodic realisation includes multiple dimensions, such as pitch, voice quality, loudness, etcetera, and constructs always vary in some of these features while they resemble each other in others. The multidimensionality of prosody and the extreme degree of variance that comes with it means that only a few researchers to date have found stable relations between given prosodic features and specific meanings or interactional functions of verbal patterns. Accordingly, quite some studies, which depart from a CxG point of view, conclude that the role of prosody is better described as a contextualisation cue rather than an intrinsic part of the constructions under scrutiny. Nonetheless, in general, construction grammarians seem to fare better with the idea that prosody *can* be part of a form–meaning pairing, while claims on gestures being part of constructions are met with more doubt and resistance (see also Nikiforidou, 2025).

This is also mirrored in recent attempts to model the interaction of gesture and sign in sign languages. I will not elaborate in detail on this body of work, as I am not an expert in the field, and the focus of this Element is on spoken languages. Note, however, that the discussion in sign linguistics touches upon very similar issues that are characteristic for the discussion on the multimodal status of construction in spoken languages, most notably the issue of obligatory components to constructions. In that vein, Schembri, Cormier, and Fenlon (2018: 13) explicitly refer to the discussion on multimodal constructions in their work on indicating verbs that represent a composite construction of a lexical sign and pointing in British Sign Language. They propose that 'indicating verbs constitute a structured composite construction of sign and co-sign gesture, similar to multimodal constructions of speech and co-speech gesture that have been proposed by gesture researchers within the framework of Construction Grammar', thereby providing evidence for candidate multimodal constructions in sign languages.

Wilcox, Martínez, and Siyavoshi (2024) do not refer to recent research in multimodal CxG, but their approach nevertheless seems relevant since they propose to abandon the discussion on sign and gesture as distinct modalities altogether (see also Lepic & Occhino, 2018). They cite Adam Kendon in arguing that 'it is time to discard the categories "gesture" and "sign" and develop a comparative semiotics of visible bodily action (kinesis) used in utterances by speakers and by signers' (Wilcox, Martínez & Siyavoshi, 2024: 84). They propose to no longer use the gesture–sign distinction but instead view utterances by signers as '"perceptible usage events" as a term that includes bodily actions that are visually perceived as well as bodily actions that produce an acoustic signal that is perceived by the auditory system' (84). This proposal seems radical at first sight, but ultimately, it ties in with a view that has long been established in gesture studies: language per se is multimodal (McNeill, 1992).

6.2.1 Interim Conclusions

After this presentation of the state of the art in multimodal CxG and the manifold approaches and areas of research, one may wonder how to proceed and perhaps even whether it is worthwhile to proceed at all. In Section 7, I will therefore shift focus to the future of the field and will not only argue that it is worthwhile to continue with the exploration of multimodal packages in use and ways of investigating whether or not they qualify as multimodal constructions, but also elaborate on some methodological considerations. These include the question of what corpora and data one might want to use, what statistical measures and methods might be fruitfully applied to solve the puzzles posed by the complexity of multimodal language use, and how we might progress on issues of big data analysis and (semi-)automatic data annotation. Finally, I will renew my plea that just as CA and other accounts of interactional language use may benefit from more large-scale studies and quantitative data analysis (Auer & Zima, 2021; Zima, 2023), CxG, and especially multimodal CxG, may profit from paying more attention to the qualitative analysis of constructions in use, which in most cases is *interactional* language use. Finally, I would like to reiterate that the questions posed and the issues raised in the field require looking beyond the boundaries of CxG, if not true interdisciplinarity. The success story of CxG as a model (see Cappelle, 2024: 8–10) is mirrored in the fact that (among others) interactional linguists have repeatedly turned to CxG in search of a model of the language system that is compatible with the nature of interactional communication. Construction grammarians, in turn, seem to be rather put off by the natural complexity of interactional language use and rarely analyse authentic, spontaneous, face-to-face interaction, despite its undisputed role in human communication and the fact that it is the natural 'home' of all constructions. I would, however, like them to trust Harvey Sacks: interactional, multimodal data may look messy at first, but there is 'order at all points' (Sacks, 1992: 486).

7 The Future: Where Do We Go from Here?

In this section, I will focus on ways to move forward and to book progress in the field. To that aim, I will concentrate on methodological issues. These include issues of data collection and analysis, data annotation, statistical analysis, and new ways of capturing and reconstructing the kinesic behaviour of language users, such as mobile eye tracking and motion capturing. We start this methodological section by focussing on the kind of data that we might want to collect and analyse to study constructs and constructions in their multimodal usage contexts.

Research in multimodal CxG stands and falls with the availability of data resources that are both large enough and of good enough quality for quantitative and qualitative analysis. The combination of both is rare. More specifically, to be able to analyse constructions in their multimodal usage contexts, we need video recordings of authentic discourse, in which interactants' bodily conduct is visible, and we need vast amounts of these recordings.[17] As the focus of multimodal CxG so far has been almost exclusively on manual gestures, researchers used data from very different sources provided that the video recordings involved speakers, whose torso was on camera so that all movements of the hands were identifiable. However, manual gestures are just one of many possible kinesic articulators that can correlate with the use of verbal constructions. Also, head movements, facial expressions, or body postures may be significant. Therefore, in order not to limit the scope of analysis to one kinesic modality a priori, on arbitrary grounds, data that allow analysing all verbal, para-verbal and non-verbal behaviour in accurate detail are desirable. This prerequisite is usually met by interaction recordings that are planned and set up for specific research purposes. However, usually, the size of such datasets is rather small (a couple of hours of recorded data) and often ethics guidelines and privacy consent forms of study participants do not allow researchers to share their recordings.[18]

This means that the size of the available high-quality data is usually too small to carry out multimodal constructional research for constructions with low token frequencies because the data do not contain enough instantiations to build data collections of significant size and to allow for statistical analysis.[19] Nonetheless, they may contain enough instantiations of constructions with medium-to-high token frequency to not only identify patterns but also allow for statistical testing. Therefore, they may nonetheless be usable for CxG research. Moreover, in contrast to the use of existing corpora, recording own data also comes with the advantage of having more control over it: including over the recording setting, participant selection, light conditions, quality of audio recording, etcetera.

In addition, technology can be used to adequately capture interactants' kinesic behaviour. This includes, for instance, the use of multiple cameras to record interactions from multiple angles, but also, for example, the use of mobile eye-tracking glasses to capture the gaze behaviour from a first-person perspective. Recent research on gaze patterns in interaction has presented

---

[17] At least, the kinesic behaviour needs to be visible in the videos to an extent that it can be analysed.

[18] Anonymizing software such as the Red Hen anonymizer may prove useful to make these data accessible for wider use, but it remains to be seen whether they have a significant impact on the common practice to not share data on human communicative behavior (and of universities and research institutes to actively prohibit making data publicly available).

[19] Of course, also very simple statistics such as frequency counts become meaningless if they are based on just a very low token number.

growing evidence that the accurate reconstruction of interactants' gaze behaviour is heavily dependent on the access to the participants' very own perspective (Zima et al., 2025). It has shown that the use of eye tracking or other methods that come as close to the participants' perspectives as possible (e.g. head-mounted GoPro cameras) are prerequisite for accurate gaze analysis. This is because gaze annotation from a bystander's perspective – that is, in ordinary video recordings – is a highly unreliable method as it relies too heavily on the equation of head direction with gaze direction (for a detailed discussion of the advantages of mobile eye tracking compared to analysing gaze from a bystander's perspective, see Zima, Auer & Rühlemann, 2025; and also Stukenbrock & Zima, 2025; Auer & Zima, 2021; Zima, 2020). However, a detailed and accurate description of gaze is mandatory to analyse its functions with respect to constructions. This is due to the fact that the temporal windows of analysis – that is, the production phase of the constructions under scrutiny – may be very short, so that accompanying meaningful gaze shifts may be very short and subtle too. This requires the availability of precise and fine-grained information on interactants' (or speakers') gaze behaviour.

Other technological devices used to conduct research on multimodal constructions are motion-capturing systems (as employed, e.g., by Mittelberg (2017) to analyse the multimodality of German *es gibt*-constructions). They provide extremely detailed and machine-readable information about the movements of study participants which allow for the detection of movement patterns. However, motion capturing may have bigger potential for follow-up experimental research on multimodal constructions that have been identified in corpora than for building up these corpora. Not only are the systems extremely expensive and therefore available to only few researchers interested in the topic, but they also require an experimental laboratory environment and are rarely used in truly interactive settings. Furthermore, recent years have seen the introduction of software packages such as OpenPose that detect motions in any video. The results are very similar to what we get from motion-capturing systems, but with the big advantages of being low cost and applicable to any video, even if it contains more than one person. This means that one no longer needs a lab infrastructure and no sensors need to be attached to the bodies of study participants. It seems obvious that in the long run, software packages such as OpenPose[20] and others, as well as the tremendous potential of using artifical intelligence for automatic gesture detection and video analysis,[21] will probably make the rather invasive method of motion capturing obsolete.

---

[20] For more information visit https://github.com/CMU-Perceptual-Computing-Lab/openpose?tab=readme-ov-file (last accessed on 18 December 2024).

[21] See also the Multidata pipeline: https://multi-data.eu/ (last accessed on 26 February 2025).

However, for the time being, the most widespread and obvious way to gather data for multimodal CxG research is to consult existing corpora and databanks. For research on English constructions, the state of the art currently is the UCLA NewsScape Library (https://tvnews.library.ucla.edu), which served as a database for almost all studies in multimodal CxG so far. It is the by far largest collection of multimodal language use that is currently available. It is based on the constant, 24/7 recording of no fewer than 300,000 news broadcasts of US broadcast stations since 2005 but also includes (selected) data that are older than that. In total, it contains roughly 400,000 hours of video data.

A similar resource is the TV News Archive (https://archive.org/details/tv), which contains 2.6 million videos of various news broadcasts. Both archives are searchable for lexical strings since the videos are aligned with the closed captions that are automatically extracted from the videos. Recent work that has made use of these resources includes, among many others, Valenzuela et al. (2020), Zima (2017a, 2017b, 2014), Uhrig (2021a, 2021b, 2022), Lehmann and Pentrel (2023), and Lehmann (2024). The unmatched amount of data that both of these archives contain allows one to retrieve a sizeable amount of multimodal usage data for just any English construction. For example, a simple search in the TV News Archive for 'all the way' delivers no fewer than 1,785,000 hits.

This does not mean that all of these nearly 1.8 million hits would be usable for multimodal CxG research, if one was even able to master this gigantic amount of data. Because the data come from all kinds of news broadcasts, it is very common for the speaker's voice to come from the background. In other words, there is no speaker on screen who is actually using the verbal construction one has searched for, and even in these cases, where the video clip contains an on-screen speaker using this particular construction, very often not all kinesic articulators are equally visible. Due to these two factors, only a fraction of the hits identified by the search engine are suitable for analysis.

Furthermore, it goes without saying that it is both impossible and unnecessary to manually scan all these data for suitable examples (see also Uhrig 2021b). Although research on constructions needs to be based on a representative data sample, it seems reasonable to assume that a collection of a couple of hundred examples usually does the job. In addition, there is a point beyond which more data no longer improves the validity of statistical models. However, the process of retrieving suitable data from such large-scale archives is time-consuming, and so is data annotation.

Depending on the research questions and hypotheses that one wants to test, data annotation can rely on rather straightforward binary coding or very detailed, multiparametric coding. Binary coding may, for instance, consist of a simple yes or no coding for whether a manual gesture accompanies a verbal construction or not. Multiparametric coding may, for instance, involve prosodic parameters such as intonational contour, pitch variations, loudness, accentuation, etcetera, alongside an application of the facial action coding scheme by Ekman and Friesen (1978), gaze patterns, head gesture uses, and many more. Also, it may involve categorial (e.g. iconic gesture, beat gesture, metaphoric gesture) and/or continuous variables (e.g. duration of gesture units). To facilitate annotation, Peter Uhrig (2021b) has successfully used automatic gesture detection algorithms (based on OpenPose), which detect not all, but a very significant part of the gestures in his NewsScape Library data. The development of new ways to automatically transcribe and annotate data is in fact progressing so rapidly that a concise description of the methods and tools would very likely be outdated by the publication of this Element. Therefore, I am not delving into the details at this point, but instead, refer to the RedHenLab website at www.redhenlab.org. Launched by Mark Turner and Francis Steen, the RedHenLab develops a vast array of tools for data annotation and analysis, mainly to be used on the NewsScape Library data.

There is no doubt that both the UCLA NewsScape Library and the TV News Archive are big steps forward for research on multimodal communication. Many research questions, especially those that in one way or another rely on a representative number of examples to run statistical tests on them, only become researchable once we have enough data at our disposal. However, a few cautious words are in order.

News broadcasts are, for a very large part, monological in nature. The use of the term 'monological' is, of course, not meant in the Bakhtinian sense; television per definition is dialogic as it is designed to address an audience. However, this audience is not physically present with the news presenter, and there is no *face-to-face* interaction. However, the archive does not only involve classic news broadcasts, but also talk shows, such as *Ellen*, *The Tonight Show*, *The Late Show*, and many others. These data involve direct *face-to-face* interactions between the show host and guests that come close(r) to authentic interactions. However, one aspect that one has to bear in mind when analysing this kind of data is the fact that the speakers (or interactants) are all well trained to speak in public and the data per definition are public discourse. This may have manifold implications for how representative the data are for private, everyday interactions. They potentially include differences in register, speech fluency, expressivity, control of emotion, and many others. Most notably, different TV genres come with different norms regarding the degree to which speakers may or may not express their own stances and emotion displays. For example, news presenters are expected to present the news rather neutrally and free of emotion. This holds to a much lesser degree for American news broadcasts than it typically holds for European ones, but there is still a noticeable difference compared to, for example, talk shows. Furthermore, news presenters prototypically sit at a table so that only their upper torso is visible on screen. Both the normative prescription to show less emotion and the bodily arrangement inhibit the display of expressive facial expressions as well as co-speech gesture use (see also Zima 2017b). This may result in lower frequencies for kinesic movements that are co-produced with constructions in these data than they are in spontaneous, naturally occurring interactions.

One problem, which, however, may be solved in the nearer future, also constitutes the fact that the queries that can be run on the data only allow one to search for verbal patterns. This means that it is not yet possible to search for a given gesture in order to study with which verbal construction that particular gesture is used. To enable these types of searches is a big desideratum, since it would not only mean a great step forward in leaving the 'verbal language bias'[22] behind, but also, we need this kind of information to calculate cross-modal collostructional strength, as Uhrig (2021b) has shown. Before I elaborate on the issue of statistics for multimodal CxG, I would like to introduce some other data resources, most notably also for languages other than English.

Another useful resource is the archive of multimodal data recordings in the CLARIN infrastructure (www.clarin.eu/resource-families/multimodal-corpora). The size of the data is not comparable to the News Archives (supra), but most of the seventeen corpora that are offered on the website contain recordings of *face-to-face* interactions. The corpora are often tagged and annotated to various degrees and, most notably, the archive contains data in languages other than English, including Frech, German, Greek, Hungarian, and others. Some corpora are publicly accessible, while others are only accessible upon request.

Furthermore, researchers working on German may consult the FOLK corpus and the Database for Spoken German of the Institute for German Language (IDS; https://agd.ids-mannheim.de/korpus_index.shtml). The FOLK corpus 'comprises audio and video recordings, transcripts, and metadata of 436 interactions with 1,381 documented speakers. The overall duration of the recordings is 364 hours and 47 minutes' (https://agd.ids-mannheim.de/FOLK_extern.shtml, last consulted on 19 December 2024). The data are searchable for lexical strings and regular expressions, but, again, not for non-verbal forms. As mentioned, this is problematic for the calculation of some statistical measures.

In Section 4, I presented different quantitative methods that have been applied to the study of multimodal constructions, and I argued that relative frequencies of

---

[22] Of course, as one of the reviewers pointed out, the verbal language bias originates in the written language bias of CxG (and all other grammar models, Linell 2009), as the study of written language naturally implies a focus restriction to verbally conveyed forms and meanings.

co-speech gesture use (or other co-occurring kinesic features) are valuable indicators for the prevalence of a multimodal package, which may or may not point towards unification of that package. However, the quantitative analysis should go beyond these frequency counts. Debras (2021), Uhrig (2021a, 2012b), Lehmann and Pentrel (2023), and Lehmann (2024) have all presented different statistical tests and measurements to establish the statistical strength of the relationship between verbal and non-verbal structures. For example, Debras (2021) has proposed using multiple correspondence analysis (Desagulier, 2017) to identify the strength of association between variables in a set of nominal categorial variables. In her analysis, these include prosodic parameters and co-speech gesture use, as well as pragmatic and interactional functions. Her analysis allows her to show that the three phonological profiles of French *je ne sais pas* (I do not know) that she studies are all strongly associated with a set of different prosodic parameters but only weakly associated with the kinesic features under scrutiny.

Lehmann and Pentrel (2023) pursued a similar objective – that is, to test the suitability of different annotated variables to predict the meaning of the constructions with which they occur (i.e. ish constructions with approximation, properties and modification meanings). To that aim, they fitted a generalised linear mixed-effects model (see also Lehmann, 2024 on 'Tell me about it'). They found that none of the kinesic features reaches a significant level in the statistical model, while the prosodic features turned out to be significant and construction specific. From this analysis, they concluded that the prosodic features are part of the constructions' forms, whereas the kinesic features are not. Both statistical procedures aim to uncover which independent variables in a set of annotated data co-occur with a given dependent variable to a statistically significant degree.

Uhrig (2021a, 2012b) proposed another approach that is based on the calculation of quantitative association between a given verbal construction and a given kinesic sign, a co-speech gesture in this case. To that aim, he carried out a collostructional analysis, as developed by Stefanowitsch and Gries (2003). This method is based on contingency tables. Hartmann and Ungerer (2023: 608) provide a very accessible explanation of the procedure as applied to lexical constructions and the calculation of the collocational strength with given items to fill an open slot within these constructions: 'For each lexical item i in a syntactic construction C with one open slot, a cross-tabulation test is computed over a 2×2 table containing a) the frequency of i in C, b) the frequency in which C is attested with any other lexical item¬i, c) the frequency of the lexical item i in all other constructions¬C, and d) the frequency of all other lexical items¬i in all other constructions¬C. In doing so, one can identify lexemes that occur with above-chance frequency in a construction.'

Table 1 Exemplary contingency table for the calculation of collostructional strength of a given verbal construction and a given gesture

	Not gesture G	**Gesture G**
Construction C	Frequency of particular gesture (G) with construction (C)	Frequency of C without gesture G
Not construction C	Frequency of G with any other construction than C	Frequency of any gesture other than G with any other construction than C

When it comes to cross-modal collostructions, the principle of the calculation stays the same, but it is significantly harder to fill in the fields of the contingency table. This is illustrated in Table 1. It shows that to calculate cross-modal collstructional strength, we do not only need the frequency with which a given construction is used together and without a particular gesture (row 2, columns 2 and 3) as well as the frequency for the use of that particular gesture with any other constructions (row 3, column 2), but also the frequency of all constructions that are used with any other gesture than the one that is relevant for the other fields of the table (row 3, column 3).

The prerequisite for such a statistical procedure thus is a fully annotated, representative dataset. The challenge, however, is not only the workload required to arrive at such a dataset, but also the very fact that it relies on solid annotation criteria that, in turn, depend on a thorough, operationalisable understanding of the nature of gesture recurrence.

At this point, the discussion on this issue comes full circle as I argued in Sections 3 and 4 that recurrence is a difficult concept in the context of complex, multivariate, multimodal data. More pessimistic readers may conclude that this is a catch-22, since a complicated theoretical issue needs to be tackled and resolved before we can book progress on the methodological front. In my view, however, this is actually unproblematic as research in multimodal CxG, such as any endeavour with the cognitive linguistic framework, calls for a bottom-up approach. This entails that we need to prioritise the work with and analysis of suitable data and the development of methods to answer our research question before we address the bigger questions on the theoretical implications for the model of CxG. I elaborate on this issue in the concluding Section 8 of this Element.

8 Concluding Remarks

This Element was dedicated to the recent development of CxG to extend its focus towards the multimodality of language use and language in use. I set the stage by first emphasising that the unimodal conception of constructions and the constructicon is at least potentially at odds with the primordial role of multimodal, *face-to-face* language use and the usage-based approach to language learning and language development. The idea that constructions may be multimodal in nature, combining verbal and non-verbal form and meaning aspects, has been raised in numerous studies over the past ten to fifteen years, with the topic gaining significantly more traction recently.

Nonetheless, the field of multimodal CxG faces several theoretical and methodological challenges and is met with quite some scepticism within the community. This, I have argued, is partly due to a conception of non-verbal behaviour as entirely ad hoc and additive to the core channel of communication – that is, the verbal channel – which is also often referred to as the 'linguistic' channel. This entails that the non-verbal modalities are conceptualised as being outside of language proper. Accordingly, it has been suggested that constructions are multimodal if and only if a given kinesic component fills an obligatory slot within a verbal construction. Prime examples of constructions that fulfil this criterion are deictic constructions such as German *so*-constructions (English: *this X*-construction as in, e.g., *the puppet is this big*), which need to be accompanied by a gesture that specifies the X-slot in order to be complete and interpretable. The current debate in the field centres around the question whether only constructions that contain slots that obligatorily need to be filled by a non-verbal element qualify as multimodal constructions or whether other ways to model multimodality within CxG are more accurate. To that aim, in Section 3, I presented different conceptions of multimodal constructions and multimodal links between constructions that coexist in the field.

This multitude of approaches was laid out in more detail in Section 4. It is split into two subsections and discusses two main approaches: frequency-based and meaning-centred perspectives. Studies that ground their arguments for or against the multimodal status of a given construction in the frequency of co-occurrence patterns of gestures, or other co-verbally occurring kinesic aspects, and verbal constructions, analyse how frequently non-verbal features accompany a specific construction in a given dataset. Most of the earlier studies in multimodal CxG report absolute and relative frequencies, but more recent studies have successfully applied more sophisticated methods of statistical data exploration. However, some scholars have argued that quantitative information alone cannot capture the full significance of the semantic-pragmatic import of non-verbal articulators, as well-informed qualitative analyses are crucial for understanding why kinesic expressive means are used in some contexts but not in others. Meaning-centred approaches therefore emphasise how gestures contribute to the meaning of constructs and utterances, challenging the traditional, form-centred perspectives of CxG.

I have repeatedly argued that to book progress in the field, it is not sufficient to look out for recurrent co-occurrences of verbal, para-verbal, or non-verbal forms, although this may be a necessary first step to take. Multimodal CxG not only hinges on close evaluations of the meaning import of kinesic forms but more broadly, it is also dependent on a thorough understanding of the complex nature of multimodal interaction and sense-making. This entails that as construction grammarians, we not only need to genuinely broaden our purely linguistic – that is, verbally centred – perspectives and take a holistic view on language (in) use but it is also essential to bear in mind that the function of non-verbal cues is not always semantically related to the meaning of the ongoing utterance (part) it co-occurs with (cf. Section 6.1 on gaze).

I have further argued that the growing interest in the identification of multimodal units in discourse is not a trend that is unique to CxG. Recent conversation analytical and interactional linguistic work has focussed on very similar issues, trying to identify recurrent configurations of verbal and non-verbal conduct in interactional data. The findings made in this line of research, as well as the issues and concerns raised, are highly relevant for multimodal CxG and therefore were presented in Section 5.

Building on this broad presentation of the state-of-the-art research in the field, Section 6 was dedicated to the future of the field. I argued that progress in the field is first and foremost dependent on the availability of suitable data. This implies that we need corpora and archives that are large enough to contain enough data to also study constructions with medium-to-low token frequency. However, quantity is not sufficient. We also need data that are of good enough quality. To this aim, I have presented resources of multimodal data that are currently used within the field. The progress in data collection and presentation, possibilities to run queries on these data, data tagging, and (semi-automatic) annotation is rapid and therefore, the good news is that this section of this Element may probably already be slightly outdated on publication day. Finally, I have also presented quantitative methods that go beyond mere frequency. Also in this respect, the development is fast and very promising.

All these recent developments within the field fuel my optimism that multimodal CxG is not only one of the newest branches of CxG but will develop in a very productive one, changing the way we conceptualise language and paying tribute to the fundamental role of multimodal language use in human communication and interaction.

References

Andrén, M. (2010). Children's gestures from 18 to 30 months. PhD thesis. Lund University: Centre for Languages and Literature.

Argyle, M. & Cook, M. (1976). *Gaze and mutual gaze.* Cambridge: Cambridge University Press.

Auer, P. (2005). Projection in interaction and projection in grammar. *Text & Talk*, **25**(1), 7–36.

Auer, P. (2021). Turn-allocation and gaze: A multimodal revision of the 'current-speaker-selects-next' rule of the turn-taking system of conversation analysis. *Discourse Studies*, **23**(2), 117–140.

Auer, P. & Zima, E. (2021). On word searches, gaze, and co-participation. *Gesprächsforschung – Online – Zeitschrift zur verbalen Interaktion*, **22**, 390–425. www.gespraechsforschung-online.de/fileadmin/dateien/heft2021/ga-auer.pdf.

Auer, P. & Zima, E. (in preparation). *Gaze aversion during answers correlates with answer complexity not preference.*

Balantani, A. (2022). Non-lexical vocalisations + 'so_was' as a multimodal package in establishing joint decisions in music rehearsals. *Language & Communication*, **87**(6), 147–160.

Barth-Weingarten. D. (2011). Response tokens in interaction. Prosody, phonetics and a visual aspect of JAJA. *Gesprächsforschung – Online – Zeitschrift zur verbalen Interaktion*, **12**, 301–370. www.gespraechsforschung-online.de/fileadmin/dateien/heft2011/ga-barth-weingarten.pdf.

Barth-Weingarten, D., Couper-Kuhlen, E. & Deppermann, A. (2020). Konstruktionsgrammatik und Prosodie: OH in englischer Alltagsinteraktion. In W. Imo & J. Lanwer (Eds.). *Prosodie und Konstruktionsgrammatik*. Berlin: De Gruyter, pp. 35–73.

Beattie, G. (1979). Contextual constraints on the floor-apportionment function of speaker-gaze in dyadic conversations. *British Journal of Social & Clinical Psychology*, **18**(4), 391–392.

Blumenthal-Dramé, A. (2012). *Entrenchment in usage-based theories: What corpus data do and do not reveal about the mind.* Berlin: Mouton de Gruyter.

Bressem, J. (2013). A linguistic perspective on the notation of form features in gestures. In C. Müller, A. Cienki, E. Fricke, S. H. Ladewig, D. McNeill & S. Teßendorf (Eds.). *Body-language-communication: An international handbook on multimodality in human interaction*. Handbooks of Linguistics and Communication Science 38.1. Berlin: Mouton De Gruyter, pp. 1079–1098.

Bressem, J. & Ladewig, S. (2011). Rethinking gesture phases: Articulatory features of gestural movement? *Semiotica*, **184**(1/4), 53–91.

Bressem, J. & Müller, C. (2017). The 'negative-assessment-construction': A multimodal pattern based on a recurrent gesture? *Linguistics Vanguard*, **3**. https://doi.org/10.1515/lingvan-2016-0053.

Bröker, S. & Zima, E. (2022). Disaffiliierende Bewertungen und Haltungsbekundungen in Erzählaktivitäten: Eine multimodale Analyse. *Linguistik Online*, **118**(6), 29–55. https://doi.org/10.13092/lo.118.9087.

Brône, G. & Zima, E. (2015). Towards a dialogic construction grammar: A corpus-based approach to ad hoc routines and resonance activation. *Cognitive Linguistics*, **25**(3), Internet-Memes S. 457–495.

Bühler, K. (1934). *Sprachtheorie: Die Darstellungsfunktion der Sprache*. Jena: Gustav Fischer.

Bülow, L., Merten, M.-L. & Johann, M. (2018). Internet-memes als Zugang zu multimodalen Konstruktionen. *Zeitschrift für Angewandte Linguistik*, **69**, 1–32. https://doi.org/10.1515/zfal-2018-0015.

Bybee, J. (2002). Sequentiality as the basis of constituent structure. In T. Givon & B. F. Malle (Eds.). *The evolution of language out of pre-language*. Amsterdam: John Benjamins, pp. 109–134.

Bybee, J. (2006). From usage to grammar: The mind's response to repetition. *Language*, **82**, 711–733.

Bybee, J. (2010). *Language, usage and cognition*. Cambridge: Cambridge University Press.

Calabria, V. & De Stefani, E. (2024). 'E anche'-prefaced other-expansions in multi-person interaction: The syntactic by-product of mutual gaze. In M. Selting & D. Barth-Weingarten (Eds.). *New perspectives in interactional linguistic research*. Amsterdam: John Benjamins, pp. 162–186.

Calbris, G. (2011). *Elements of meaning in gesture*. Amsterdam: John Benjamins.

Cappelle B. (2024). *Can construction grammar be proven wrong?* Cambridge: Cambridge University Press.

Cienki, A. (2008). Why study metaphor and gesture? In C. Müller & A. Cienki (Eds.). *Metaphor and gesture*. Amsterdam: John Benjamins, pp. 5–26.

Cienki, A. (2012). Usage events of spoken language and the symbolic units we (may) abstract from them. In J. Badio & K. Kosecki (Eds.). *Cognitive processes in language*. Bern: Peter Lang, pp. 149–158.

Cienki, A. (2013). Image schemas and mimetic schemas in cognitive linguistics and gesture studies. *Review of Cognitive Linguistics*, **11**(2), 417–432.

Cienki, A. (2015). Spoken language usage events. *Language & Cognition*, **7**, 499–514.

Cienki, A. (2016). Cognitive linguistics, gesture studies, and multimodal communication. *Cognitive Linguistics*, **27**(4), 603–618.

Cienki, A. (2017). Utterance construction grammar (UCxG) and the variable multimodality of constructions. *Linguistics Vanguard*, **3**. https://doi/10.1515/lingvan-2016-0048.

Cienki, A. & Müller, C. (2008). Metaphor, gesture, and thought. In R. Gibbs (Ed.). *Metaphor and thought*. Cambridge: Cambridge University Press, pp. 483–501.

Cohn, N. & Schilperoord, J. (2024). *A multimodal language faculty: A cognitive framework for human communication*. London: Bloomsbury.

Cooperrider, K. (2009). Book review of Nicholas J. Enfield & Stephen C. Levinson (Eds.). (2006). *Roots of human sociality: Culture, cognition and interaction*. Oxford: Berg. *Gesture*, **9**(3), 373–380.

Croft, W. (2001). *Radical construction grammar: Syntactic theory in typological perspective*. Oxford: Oxford University Press.

Cuyckens, H. & Zawada, B. (2001) Introduction. In H. Cuyckens & B. Zawada (Eds.). *Polysemy in cognitive linguistics*. Amsterdam: John Benjamins, pp. ix–xxvii.

Dąbrowska, E. (2012). Different speakers, different grammars: Individual differences in native language attainment. *Linguistic Approaches to Bilingualism*, **2**(3), 219–253. https://doi.org/10.1075/lab.2.3.01dab.

Dancygier B. & Vandelanotte, L. (2017). Internet memes as multimodal constructions. *Cognitive Linguistics*, **28**(3), 565–598. https://doi.org/10.1515/cog-2017-0074.

Debras, C. (2021). Multimodal profiles of *je (ne) sais pas* in spoken French. *Journal of Pragmatics*, **182**(1), 42–62.

Deppermann, A. (2011). Konstruktionsgrammatik und Interaktionale Linguistik: Affinitäten, Komplementaritäten und Diskrepanzen. In A. Lasch & A. Ziem (Eds.). *Konstruktionsgrammatik III: Aktuelle Fragen und Lösungsansätze*. Tubingen: Stauffenburg, pp. 205–238.

Deppermann, A. (2012). How does 'cognition' matter to the analysis of talk-in-interaction? *Language Sciences*, **34**(6), 746–767.

Desagulier, G. (2017). *Corpus linguistics and statistics with R*. Cham: Springer. https://doi.org/10.1007/978-3-319-64572-8.

Diessel, H. (1999). *Demonstratives: Form, function, and grammaticalization*. Amsterdam: John Benjamins.

Diessel, H. (2006). Demonstratives, joint attention, and the emergence of grammar. *Cognitive Linguistics*, **17**(4), 463–489. https://doi.org/10.1515/COG.2006.015.

Diessel, H. (2023). *The constructicon: Taxonomies and networks.* Cambridge: Cambridge University Press.

Divjak, D. (2019). *Frequency in language: Memory, attention and learning.* Cambridge: Cambridge University Press.

Divjak, D. & Caldwell-Harris, C. (2015). Frequency and entrenchment. In E. Dąbrowska & D. Divjak (Eds.). *Handbook of cognitive linguistics.* Berlin: De Gruyter, pp. 53–75.

Droste, P. & Günthner, S. (2020). 'Das mAchst du bestimmt AUCH du': Zum Zusammenspiel grammatischer, prosodischer und sequenzieller Aspekte syntaktisch desintegrierter du-Formate. In W. Imo & J. Lanwer (Eds.). *Prosodie und Konstruktionsgrammatik.* Berlin: De Gruyter, pp. 75–109.

Droste, P. & Günthner, S. (2021). Enacting 'being with you': Vocative uses of *du* ('you') in German everyday interaction. *Pragmatics,* **31**(1), 87–113. https://doi.org/10.1075/prag.19030.dro.

Ekman, P. & Friesen, W. V. (1978). *Facial action coding system.* Palo Alto, CA: Consulting Psychologist Press.

Enfield, N. (2009). *The anatomy of meaning: Speech, gesture, and composite utterances.* Cambridge: Cambridge University Press.

Feyaerts, K., Brône G. & Oben, B. (2017). Multimodality in interaction. In B. Dancygier, (Ed.). *The Cambridge handbook of cognitive linguistics.* Cambridge: Cambridge University Press, pp. 1535–1565.

Feyaerts, K., Brône, G., Sambre, P., Oben, B., Schoonjans, S. & Zima, E. (2014). *Accounting for multimodality in construction grammar.* Talk at DGKL 6, Nuremberg-Erlangen, October.

Forceville, C. (2008). Metaphor in pictures and multimodal representations. In R. Gibbs (Ed.). *The Cambridge handbook of metaphor and thought.* Cambridge: Cambridge University Press, pp. 462–482.

Fried, M. & Nikiforidou, K. (Eds.). (2025). *Multimodal communication from a construction grammar perspective.* Amsterdam: John Benjamins.

Givón, T. (1984). Universals of discourse structure and second language acquisition. In W. E. Rutherford (Ed.). *Language universals and second language acquisition.* Amsterdam: John Benjamins, pp. 109–136.

Glenberg A. M., Schroeder J. L. & Robertson D. A. (1998). Averting the gaze disengages the environment and facilitates remembering. *Memory & Cognition,* **26**, 651–658.

Goldberg, A. (1998). Patterns of experience in patterns of language. In M. Tomasello (Ed.). *The new psychology of language: Cognitive and functional approaches to language structure.* Mahwah, NJ: Lawrence Erlbaum Associates, pp. 203–219.

Goldberg, A. (2003). Constructions: A new theoretical approach to language. *Trends in Cognitive Science*, **7**, 219–224.

Goldberg, A. (2019). *Explain me this: Creativity, competition, and the partial productivity of constructions*. Princeton, NJ: Princeton University Press.

Goodwin, Ch. (1980). Restarts, pauses, and the achievement of a state of mutual gaze at turn-beginning. *Sociological Inquiry*, **50**(3–4), 272–302.

Goodwin, Ch. (1981). *Conversational organization: Interaction between speakers and hearers*. London: Academic Press.

Goodwin, Ch. (2003). The power of Schegloff's work. In L. Prevignano & P. J. Thibault (Eds.). *Discussing conversation analysis: The work of Emanuel A. Schegloff*. New York: John Benjamins, pp. 57–64.

Goodwin, M. H. & Goodwin, Ch. (1986). Gesture and coparticipation in the activity of searching for a word. *Semiotica*, **62**(1–2), 51–75.

Gras, P. & Elvira-García, W. (2021). The role of intonation in construction grammar: On prosodic constructions. *Journal of Pragmatics*, **180**, 232–247. https://doi.org/10.1016/j.pragma.2021.05.010.

Gumperz, J. J. (1982). *Discourse strategies*. Cambridge: Cambridge University Press.

Gumperz, J. J. (1992). Contextualization and understanding. In A. Duranti & Ch. Goodwin (Eds.). *Rethinking context: Language as an interpretative phenomenon*. Cambridge: Cambridge University Press, pp. 229–252.

Günthner, S. (2011). Between emergence and sedimentation: Projecting constructions in German interactions. In P. Auer & S. Pfänder (Eds.). *Constructions: Emerging and emergent*. Berlin: De Gruyter, pp. 156–185.

Haddington, P. (2006). The organization of gaze and assessments as resources for stance taking. *Text & Talk*, **26**, 281–328.

Hampe, B., Mittelberg, I., Uhrig, P. & Turner, M. (2018). There-constructions 'in the wild': A quantitative pilot study of multimodal conversational data. 8th International Conference of the German Cognitive Linguistics Association (DGKL8), Koblenz.

Harrison, S. M. (2009). Grammar, gesture, and cognition: The case of negation in English. Bordeaux: Université Michel de Montaigne Bordeaux 3 dissertation.

Hartmann S. & Ungerer, T. (2023). Attack of the snowclones: A corpus-based analysis of extravagant formulaic patterns. *Journal of Linguistics* **60**(3), 599–634. https://doi.org/10.1017/S002222672300011.

Hayashi, M. (2005). Joint turn construction through language and the body: Notes on embodiment in coordinated participation in situated activities. *Semiotica*, **156**, 21–53. https://doi.org/10.1515/semi.2005.2005.156.21.

Heath, Ch. (1993). Gesture's discreet tasks multiple relevancies in visual conduct and in the contextualisation of language. In P. Auer & A. Di Luzio (Eds.). *The contextualization of language*. Amsterdam: John Benjamins, pp. 101–128.

Hilpert, M. (2013). *Constructional change in English: Developments in allomorphy, word formation, and syntax*. Cambridge: Cambridge University Press.

Hilpert, M. (2014). *Construction grammar and its application to English*. Edinburgh: Edinburgh University Press.

Hilpert, M. (2021). *Ten lectures on diachronic construction grammar*. Leiden: Brill.

Hinell, J. (2018). The multimodal marking of aspect: The case of five periphrastic auxiliary constructions in North American English. *Cognitive Linguistics*, **29**(4), 773–806.

Ho, S., Foulsham, T. & Kingstone, A. (2015). Speaking and listening with the eyes: Gaze signaling during dyadic interactions. *PLOS ONE*, **10**(8): e0136905. https://doi.org/10.1371/journal.pone.0136905.

Hoffmann, T. (2013). Abstract phrasal and clausal constructions. In G. Trousdale & T. Hoffmann (Eds.). *The Oxford handbook of construction grammar*. Cambridge: Cambridge University Press, pp. 307–328.

Hoffmann, T. (2017). Multimodal constructs – multimodal constructions? The role of constructions in the working memory. *Linguistics Vanguard*, **3**. https://doi.org/10.1515/lingvan-2016-0042.

Holler, J., Kendrick, K. & Levinson, S. C. (2018). Processing language in face-to-face conversation: Questions with gestures get faster responses. *Psychonomic Bulletin & Review* **25**(5), 1900–1908.

Hopper, P. (1998). Emergent grammar. In M. Tomasello (Ed.). *The new psychology of language*. Mahwah, NJ: Erlbaum, pp. 155–175.

Imo, W. (2011). Cognitions are not observable – but their consequences are: Mögliche Aposiopese-Konstruktionen in der gesprochenen Alltagssprache. *Gesprächsforschung – Online-Zeitschrift zur verbalen Interaktion*, **12**, 265–300.

Imo, W. & Lanwer, J. (Eds.) (2020). *Prosodie und Konstruktionsgrammatik*. Berlin: De Gryuter.

Janda, L. (2013) (Ed.). *Cognitive linguistics: The quantitative turn*. Berlin: Mouton de Gryuter.

Karadöller, D. Z., Sümer, B. & Özyürek, A. (2024). First-language acquisition in a multimodal language framework: Insights from speech, gesture, and sign. *First Language*, **0**, 1–38. https://doi.org/10.1177/01427237241290678.

Kärkkäinen, E. & Thompson, S. (2018). Language and bodily resources: 'Response packages' in response to polar questions in English. *Journal of Pragmatics*, **123**, 220–238.

Keevallik, L. (2013). The interdependence of bodily demonstrations and clausal syntax. *Research on Language and Social Interaction*, **46**(1), 1–21.

Keevallik, L. (2020). Multimodal noun phrases. In T. Ono & S. Thompson (Eds.). *The 'noun phrase' across languages: An emergent unit in interaction*. Amsterdam: John Benjamins, pp. 153–176.

Kendon, A. (1967). Some functions of gaze direction in social interaction. *Acta Psychologica*, **26**, 22–63.

Kendon, A. (1980). Gesture and speech: Two aspects of the process of utterance. In M. R. Key (Ed.). *Non-verbal communication and language*. The Hague: Mouton, pp. 207–227.

Kendon, A. (2004). *Gesture: Visible action as utterance*. Cambridge: Cambridge University Press.

Kendon, A. (2015). Gesture and sign: Utterance uses of visible bodily action. In K. Allen (Ed.). *The Routledge handbook of linguistics*. London: Routledge, pp. 33–46.

Kendrick, K. & Holler, J. (2017). Gaze direction signals response preference in conversation. *Research on Language and Social Interaction*, **50**(1), 12–32.

Kendrick, K. H., Holler, J. & Levinson, S. C. (2023). Turn-taking in human face-to-face interaction is multimodal: Gaze direction and manual gestures aid the coordination of turn transitions. *Philosophical Transactions of the Royal Society B: Biological Sciences*, **378**(1875). https://doi.org/10.1098/rstb.2021.0473.

Kidwell, M. (2006). 'Calm down!' The role of gaze in the interactional management of hysteria by the police. *Discourse Studies*, **8**(6), 745–770.

Kövesces, Z. (2010). *Metaphor: A practical introduction*. Oxford: Oxford University Press.

Ladewig, S. (2011). Putting the cyclic gesture on a cognitive basis. *CogniTextes*, **6**, https://doi.org/10.4000/cognitextes.406.

Ladewig, S. (2020). *Integrating gestures: The dimension of multimodality in cognitive grammar*. Berlin: De Gruyter Mouton.

Laner, B. (2025). Mobile stance-taking in nature: An exploration of gaze patterns during assessments of objects in nature. *Frontiers in Psychology*, **15**. https://doi.org/10.3389/fpsyg.2024.461123.

Langacker, R. W. (1987). *Foundations of cognitive grammar: Theoretical prerequisites*. Stanford, CA: Stanford University Press.

Langacker, R. W. (2001). Discourse in cognitive grammar. *Cognitive Linguistics*, **12**(2), 143–188.

Langacker, R. W. (2008). Metaphoric gesture and cognitive linguistics. In A. Cienki & C. Müller (Eds.). *Metaphor and gesture*. Amsterdam: John Benjamins, pp. 249–251.

Lanwer, J. (2017). Apposition: A multimodal construction? The multimodality of linguistic constructions in the light of usage-based theory. *Linguistics Vanguard*, **3**. https://doi.org/10.1515/lingvan-2016-0071.

Lanwer, J. (2020). Appositive Syntax oder appositive Prosodie? In W. Imo & J. Lanwer (Eds.). *Prosodie und Konstruktionsgrammatik*. Berlin: De Gruyter, pp. 233–281.

Lasch, A. (2020). Semantically motivated constructions in a semantically motivated constructicon. Talk at Constructing a Constructicon. Trient, May.

Lehmann, C. (2024a). Multimodal constructions revisited: Testing the strength of association between spoken and non-spoken features of Tell me about it. *Cognitive Linguistics*, **35**(3), 407–437.

Lehmann, C. (2024b). What makes a multimodal construction? Evidence for a prosodic mode in spoken English. *Frontiers in Communication*, **9**. https://doi.org/10.3389/fcomm.2024.1338844.

Lehmann, C. & Pentrel, M. (2023). Multimodal-ish: Prosodic and kinesic aspects of bounded and free uses of ish. *Language and Cognition*, **16**(1), 1–31. https://doi.org/10.1017/langcog.2023.

Lepic, R. & Occhino, C. (2018). A construction morphology approach to sign language analysis. In G. Booij (Ed.). *The construction of words: Studies in morphology*, vol. 4. Cham: Springer, pp. 141–172. https://doi.org/10.1007/978-3-319-74394-3_6.

Linell, P. (2009). *Rethinking language, mind, and world dialogically*. Charlotte, NC: Information Age.

Marandin, J.-M. (2006). Contours as constructions. *Constructions*. https://doi.org/10.24338/cons-448.

Masini, F., Combei C. R. & Cicchirillo, R. (in press). The prosody of list constructions. In K. Nikiforidou & M. Fried (Eds.). *Multimodal communication from a construction grammar perspective*. Amsterdam: John Benjamins, pp. 116–151.

McNeill, D. (1985). So you think gestures are non-verbal? *Psychological Review*, **92**(3), 350–371.

McNeill, D. (1992). *Hand and mind: What gestures reveal about thought*. Chicago, IL: University of Chicago Press.

Meyer, C. (2016). Face-to-face communication. In K. Bruhn Jensen, T. R. Craig, J. Pooley & E. Rothenbuhler (Eds.). *The international encyclopedia of communication theory and philosophy*. Hoboken, NJ: John Wiley and Sons, pp. 1–9.

Mittelbeg, I. (2006). *Metaphor and metonymy in language and gesture: Discourse evidence for multimodal models of grammar.* PhD dissertation, Cornell University. Published online, Ann Arbor, MI: ProQuest/UMI.

Mittelberg, I. (2017). Multimodal existential constructions in German: Manual actions of giving as experiential substrate for grammatical and gestural patterns. *Linguistics Vanguard*, 3. https://doi.org/10.1515/lingvan-2016-0047.

Mittelberg, I. (2019). Visuo-kinetic signs are inherently metonymic: How embodied metonymy motivates form, function and schematic patterns in gesture. *Frontiers in Psychology*, https://doi.org/10.3389/fpsyg.2019.00254.

Mondada, L. (2014). The local constitution of multimodal resources for social interaction. *Journal of Pragmatics*, **65**, 137–156.

Mondada, L. (2024). Requesting in shop encounters. In M. Selting & D. Barth-Weingarten (Eds.). *New perspectives in interactional linguistic research.* Amsterdam: John Benjamins, pp. 278–309.

Müller, C. (2008). *Metaphors dead and alive, sleeping and waking: A dynamic view.* Chicago, IL: Chicago University Press.

Nikiforidou, K. (2025). Multimodality, conventionality and inheritance in dialogic constructions. In K. Nikiforidou & M. Fried (Eds.). *Multimodal communication from a construction grammar perspective.* Amsterdam: John Benjamins, pp. 38–68.

Nikiforidou, K. & Fried, M. (Eds.). (2025). *Multimodal communication from a construction grammar perspective.* Amsterdam: John Benjamins,

Ningelgen, J. & Auer, P. (2017). Is there a multimodal construction based on non-deictic *so* in German? *Linguistics Vanguard*, **3**. https://doi.org/10.1515/lingvan-2016-0051.

Ogden, R. (2010). Prosodic constructions in making complaints. In D. Barth-Weingarten, E. Reber & M. Selting (Eds.). *Prosody in interaction.* Amsterdam: John Benjamins, pp. 81–104.

Pagán-Cánovas, C. & Valenzuela, J. (2017). Timelines and multimodal constructions: Facing new challenges. *Linguistics Vanguard*, **3**. https://doi.org/10.1515/lingvan-2016-0087.

Pagán-Cánovas, C., Valenzuela, J., Alcaraz-Carrión, D., Olzá, I. & Ramscar, M. (2020). Quantifying the speech–gesture relation with massive multimodal datasets: Informativity in time expressions. *PloS ONE*, **15**(6), e0233892. https://doi.org/10.1371/journal.pone.0233892.

Pekarek Doehler, S. (2016). More than an epistemic hedge: French *je sais pas* 'I don't know' as a resource for the sequential organization of turns and actions. *Journal of Pragmatics*, **106**, 148–162.

Pekarek Doehler, S. (2019). At the interface of grammar and the body: *Chais pas* ('dunno') as a resource for dealing with lack of recipient response. *Research on Language and Social Interaction*, **52**(4), 1–23.

Pekarek Doehler, S. (2022). Multimodal action formats for managing preference: *Chais pas* 'dunno' plus gaze conduct in dispreferred responses to questions. *Journal of Pragmatics*, **197**(1), 81–99.

Pekarek Doehler, S., Polak-Yitzhaki, H., Li, X., Stoenica, I.-M., Havlík, M. & Keevallik, L. (2022). Multimodal assemblies for prefacing a dispreferred response: A cross-linguistic analysis. *Frontiers in Communication*, **12**(2021). www.frontiersin.org/articles/10.3389/fpsyg.2021.689275/full.

Perniss, P. (2018). Why we should study multimodal language. *Frontiers in Psychology*, **9**. www.frontiersin.org/journals/psychology/articles/10.3389/fpsyg.2018.01109.

Põldvere, N. & Paradis, C. (2020). 'What and then a little robot brings it to you?' The reactive what-x construction in spoken dialogue. *English Language & Linguistics*, **24**(2): 307–332.

Reber, E. (2012). *Affectivity in interaction: Sound objects in English*. Amsterdam: John Benjamins.

Sacks, H. (1992). *Lectures on conversation*, vols. 1 & 2. Oxford: Basil Blackwell.

Sacks, H., Schegloff, E. A. & Jefferson, G. (1974). A simplest systematics for the organization of turn-taking for conversation. *Language*, **50**(4), 696–735.

Sadat-Tehrani, N. (2010). An intonational construction. *Constructions*, **5**. https://doi.org/10.24338/cons-451.

Sanaz, M. J. (2013). Multimodality and cognitive linguistics. *Review of Cognitive Linguistics*, **11**(2), 227–235.

Schegloff, E. A. (1987). Analyzing single episodes of interaction: An exercise in conversation analysis. *Social Psychology Quarterly*, **50**(2), 101–114.

Schegloff, E. A. (1997). Narrative analysis thirty years later. In M. Bamberg (Ed.). Oral versions of personal experience: Three decades of narrative analysis. *Journal of Narrative and Life History*, **7**(1–4), 97–106.

Schembri, A., Kearsy Cormier, K. & Fenlon, J. (2018). Indicating verbs as typologically unique constructions: Reconsidering verb 'agreement' in sign languages. *Glossa: A journal of general linguistics*, **3**(1):89, 1–40. https://doi.org/10.5334/gjgl.468.

Schilperoord, J. & Cohn, N. (2022). Before: Unimodal linguistics. After: Multimodal linguistics. A parallel architecture account of a multimodal construction. *Cognitive Semantics*, **8**(1), 109–140. https://doi.org/10.1163/23526416-bja10025.

Schmid, H.-J. (2007). Entrenchment, salience and basic levels. In D. Geeraerts & H. Cuyckens (Eds.). *The Oxford handbook of cognitive linguistics*. Oxford: Oxford University Press, pp. 117–138.

Schmid, H.-J. (2014). *Entrenchment, memory and automaticity: The psychology of linguistic knowledge and language learning*. Berlin: Mouton de Gruyter.

Schmid, H.-J. (2013). Constructionist challenges and the entrenchment-and-conventionalization model. Manuscript retrieved from https://osf.io/v7j3n.

Schoonjans, S. (2017). Multimodal construction grammar issues are construction grammar issues. *Linguistics Vanguard*, 3. https://doi.org/10.1515/lingvan-2016-0050.

Schoonjans, S. (2018). *Modalpartikeln als multimodale Konstruktionen: Eine korpusbasierte Kookkurrenzanalyse von Modalpartikeln und Gestik im Deutschen*. Berlin: Mouton de Gruyter.

Silverstein, M. (1976). Shifters, linguistic categories, and cultural description. In K. H. Basso & H. A. Selby (Eds.). *Meaning in anthropology*. Albuquerque: University of New Mexico Press, pp. 1–55.

Steen, F. F., Hougaard, A., Joo, J., Olza, I., Pagán Cánovas, C., Pleshakova, A., Ray, S., Uhrig, P., Valenzuela, J., Woźny, J. & Turner, M. (2018). Toward an infrastructure for data-driven multimodal communication research. *Linguistics Vanguard*, **4**(1). https://doi.org/10.1515/lingvan-2017-0041.

Stefanowitsch, A. & Gries, St. (2003). Collostructions: Investigating the interaction of words and constructions. *International Journal of Corpus Linguistics*, **8**(2), 209–253.

Stivers, T. (2008). Stance, alignment, and affiliation during storytelling: When nodding is a token of affiliation. *Research on Language and Social Interaction*, **41**(1), 31–57. https://doi.org/10.1080/08351810701691123.

Streeck, J. (1993). Gesture as communication I: Its coordination with gaze and speech, *Communication Monographs*, **60**(4), 275–299.

Streeck, J. & Hartge U. (1992). Previews: Gestures at the transition place. In P. Auer & A. Di Luzio (Eds.). *The contextualization of language*. Amsterdam: John Benjamins, pp. 135–158.

Stukenbrock, A. (2010). Überlegungen zu einem multimodalen Verständnis der gesprochenen Sprache am Beispiel deiktischer Verwendungsweisen des Ausdrucks 'so'. *InLiSt: Interaction and Linguistic Structures*, **47**, 1–23.

Stukenbrock, A. (2015). *Deixis in der face-to-face-Interaktion*, Berlin: De Gruyter.

Stukenbrock, A. (2020). Mit Blick auf die Geste: Multimodale Verfestigungen in der Interaktion. In B. Weidner, K. König, L. Wegner & W. Imo (Eds.).

Verfestigungen in der Interaktion: Konstruktionen, sequenzielle Muster, kommunikative Gattungen. Berlin: De Gruyter, pp. 233–263.

Stukenbrock, A. (2021). Multimodal gestalts and their change over time: Is routinization also grammaticalization? *Frontiers in Communication*, **6**, 662240. https://doi.org/10.3389/fcomm.2021.662240.

Stukenbrock, A. & Zima, E. (2025). Introduction: Mobile eye tracking for the study of gaze in social interaction. In A. Stukenbrock & E. Zima (Eds.). *Mobile eyetracking: New avenues for the study of gaze in social interaction*. Amsterdam: John Benjamins, pp. 1–21.

Tomasello, M. (2003). *Constructing a language: A usage-based theory of language acquisition*. Cambridge, MA: Harvard University Press.

Traugott, E. C. & Trousdale, G. (2013). *Constructionalization and constructional changes*. Oxford: Oxford University Press.

Turner, J. (2002). *Face to face: Towards a sociological theory of interpersonal behavior*. Stanford, CA: Stanford University Press.

Uhrig, P. (2021a). Multimodal communication in construction grammar. Talk at Abralin AO Vivo. https://aovivo.abralin.org/en/lives/peter-uhrig-2, last retrieved on 21 November 2024.

Uhrig, P. (2021b). Large-scale multimodal corpus linguistics: The big data turn. Erlangen: Friedrich-Alexander-Universität Erlangen-Nürnberg, Habilitation thesis.

Uhrig, P. (2022). Hand gestures with verbs of throwing: Collostructions, style and metaphor. In B. Hampe & A. Binanzer (Eds.). *Yearbook of the German Association of Cognitive Linguistics*, vol. 10. Berlin: De Gruyter, pp. 99–120.

Ungerer, T. & Hartmann, S. (2023). *Constructionist approaches*. Cambridge: Cambridge University Press.

Vlenzuela, J., Pagán Cánovas, C., Olza, I. & Alcaraz Carrión, D. (2020). Gesturing in the wild: Spontaneous gestures co-occurring with temporal demarcative expressions provide evidence for a flexible mental timeline. *Review of Cognitive Linguistics*, **18**(2), 289–315.

Verhagen, A. (2021). *Construction grammar, multimodal communication, and design features of language: Preliminaries to a coherent research program*. Athens, SLE conference, 30 August–3 September.

Ward, N. G. (2019). *The prosodic patterns of English conversation*. Cambridge: Cambridge University Press.

Wilcox, S., Martínez, R. & Siyavoshi, S. (2024). *Signed language and cognitive grammar*. Cambridge: Cambridge University Press.

Ziem, A. (2017). Do we really need a multimodal construction grammar? *Linguistics Vanguard*, **3**. https://doi.org/10.1515/lingvan-2016-0095.

Zima, E. (2014). Gibt es multimodale Konstruktionen? Eine Studie zu [V(motion) in circles] und [all the way from X PREP Y]. *Gesprächsforschung: Online Zeitschrift zur verbalen Interaktion*, **15**, 1–48.

Zima, E. (2017a). On the multimodality of [all the way from X PREP Y]. *Linguistics Vanguard*, **3**. https://doi.org/10.1515/lingvan-2016-0055.

Zima, E. (2017b). Multimodal constructional resemblance: The case of English circular motion constructions. In F. Ruiz de Mendoza, A. Luzondo & P. Pérez-Sobrino (Eds.). *Constructing families of constructions*. Amsterdam: John Benjamins, pp. 301–337.

Zima, E. (2020). Gaze and recipient feedback in triadic storytelling activities. *Discourse Processes*, **57**(9), 725–748.

Zima, E. (2023). Gesprächsanalytische und kognitiv-linguistische Studien zur Rolle von Blick und ko-verbaler Gestik in der sozialen Interaktion. Habilitation thesis. University of Freiburg.

Zima, E. (2025). Construction grammar and gesture. In K. Nikiforidou & M. Fried (Eds.). *Cambridge handbook of construction grammar*. Cambridge: Cambridge University Press, pp. 384–404.

Zima, E., Auer, P. & Rühlemann, C. (2025). Why multimodal interaction research on gaze needs mobile eyetracking. In E. Zima & A. Stukenbrock (Eds.). *Mobile eyetracking: New avenues for the study of gaze in social interaction*. Amsterdam: John Benjamins, pp. 24–66.

Zima, E. & Bergs, A. (2017). Multimodality and construction grammar. *Linguistics Vanguard*, **3**. https://doi.org/10.1515/lingvan-2016–1006/html.

Construction Grammar

Thomas Hoffmann
Catholic University of Eichstätt-Ingolstadt

Thomas Hoffmann is Full Professor and Chair of English Language and Linguistics at the Catholic University of Eichstätt-Ingolstadt as well as Furong Scholar Distinguished Chair Professor of Hunan Normal University. His main research interests are usage-based Construction Grammar, language variation and change and linguistic creativity. He has published widely in international journals such as *Cognitive Linguistics*, *English Language and Linguistics*, and *English World-Wide*. His monographs *Preposition Placement in English* (2011) and *English Comparative Correlatives: Diachronic and Synchronic Variation at the Lexicon-Syntax Interface* (2019) were both published by Cambridge University Press. His textbook on *Construction Grammar: The Structure of English* (2022) as well as an Element on *The Cognitive Foundation of Post-colonial Englishes: Construction Grammar as the Cognitive Theory for the Dynamic Model* (2021) have also both been published with Cambridge University Press. He is also co-editor (with Graeme Trousdale) of *The Oxford Handbook of Construction Grammar* (2013, Oxford University Press).

Alexander Bergs
Osnabrück University

Alexander Bergs joined the Institute for English and American Studies at Osnabrück University, Germany, in 2006 when he became Full Professor and Chair of English Language and Linguistics. His research interests include, among others, language variation and change, constructional approaches to language, the role of context in language, the syntax/pragmatics interface, and cognitive poetics. His works include several authored and edited books (*Social Networks and Historical Sociolinguistics*, *Modern Scots*, *Contexts and Constructions*, *Constructions and Language Change*), a short textbook on *Synchronic English Linguistics*, one on *Understanding Language Change* (with Kate Burridge) and the two-volume *Handbook of English Historical Linguistics* (ed. with Laurel Brinton; now available as five-volume paperback) as well as more than fifty papers in high-profile international journals and edited volumes. Alexander Bergs has taught at the Universities of Düsseldorf, Bonn, Santiago de Compostela, Wisconsin-Milwaukee, Catania, Vigo, Thessaloniki, Athens, and Dalian and has organized numerous international workshops and conferences.

About the Series

Construction Grammar is the leading cognitive theory of syntax. The present Elements series will survey its theoretical building blocks, show how Construction Grammar can capture various linguistic phenomena across a wide range of typologically different languages, and identify emerging frontier topics from a theoretical, empirical and applied perspective.

Cambridge Elements

Construction Grammar

Elements in the Series

The Constructicon: Taxonomies and Networks
Holger Diessel

Constructionist Approaches: Past, Present, Future
Tobias Ungerer and Stefan Hartmann

Copilots for Linguists: AI, Constructions, and Frames
Tiago Timponi Torrent, Thomas Hoffmann, Arthur Lorenzi Almeida
and Mark Turner

Can Construction Grammar Be Proven Wrong?
Bert Cappelle

Constructions and Compositionality: Cognitive and Computational Explorations
Giulia Rambelli

The Meaning of Constructions
Benoît Leclercq and Cameron Morin

Unrealized Arguments and the Grammar of Context
Rui P. Chaves, Paul Kay and Laura A. Michaelis

Multimodal Construction Grammar
Elisabeth Zima

A full series listing is available at: www.cambridge.org/EICG

For EU product safety concerns, contact us at Calle de José Abascal, 56–1º,
28003 Madrid, Spain or eugpsr@cambridge.org.

www.ingramcontent.com/pod-product-compliance
Ingram Content Group UK Ltd.
Pitfield, Milton Keynes, MK11 3LW, UK
UKHW021814170925
462995UK00021B/754